The Iowa Lakeside Laboratory

A BUR OAK BOOK

Holly Carver, series editor

The Iowa Lakeside Laboratory

* *

a century of discovering the nature of nature

Michael J. Lannoo

* *

UNIVERSITY OF IOWA PRESS IOWA CITY

University of Iowa Press, Iowa City 52242
Copyright © 2012 by the University of Iowa Press
www.uiowapress.org
Printed in the United States of America

Design by Omega Clay

The University of Iowa Press is a member of Green Press Initiative and is committed to preserving natural resources.

Printed on acid-free paper

LIBRARY OF CONGRESS CATALOGING-IN-PUBLICATION DATA
Lannoo, Michael J.
The Iowa Lakeside Laboratory: a century of discovering the nature of nature / by Michael J. Lannoo.
  p.   cm.—(A Bur oak book)
Includes bibliographical references and index.
ISBN 978-1-60938-121-9, 1-60938-121-1 (pbk)
ISBN 978-1-60938-139-4, 1-60938-139-4 (ebook)
1. Iowa Lakeside Laboratory—History. 2. Ecology—Research—Iowa—History. 3. Natural history—Research—Iowa—History. 4. Conservation biology—Research—Iowa—History. 5. Nature study—Iowa—History. 6. Naturalists—Iowa—Biography. 7. Iowa Lakeside Laboratory—Biography. I. Title.
QH105.I8L34 2012
577.072'109777—dc23   2012007452

Photo of Thomas H. Macbride on p. vi courtesy of the Iowa Lakeside Library.

Dedicated to the alumni, faculty, and staff of the Iowa Lakeside Laboratory, who know why, or should, and to the Friends of Lakeside Lab, who have never doubted

Thomas H. Macbride a few days before his death in 1934.

· ·

The Lakeside Laboratory shall afford to all interested, for once at least a chance to see the real world, nature alive, accomplishing her miracles in their own silent splendor, often needing not, for the student's appreciation, the voice of interpreter or teacher.

—THOMAS H. MACBRIDE, 1909

The basic reason for Iowa Lakeside Laboratory was that typical field conditions cannot be brought to the laboratory, hence the laboratory must be brought to the field.

—IOWA STATE BOARD OF EDUCATION (REGENTS), 1947

contents

1 The Spirit

4 Something Heavy in the Midwestern Air

8 An Opportunity of Magnificent Possibilities

11 A Brief History of Field Stations

14 The Factors of Ecology Are All Here

20 The Iowa Lakeside Laboratory as a Student Sees It
   by Maud Brown, 1910

23 The Victorians, 1909–1932

41 Hard Times and Stone Labs, 1932–1947

47 Classical State Universities versus Land-grant Institutions

49 A Regents Institution, 1947–2007

67 The Friends of Lakeside Lab
   by Jane Shuttleworth

70 A Regents Resource Center, 2007–Present

75 Resurrecting Natural History

81 Acknowledgments

83 Appendixes

93 Bibliography

95 Index

The Iowa Lakeside Laboratory

the spirit

WHAT IS IT about these old stone labs? Massive glacial erratics arranged using some form of lost art to frame the narrow doors and large banks of windows and to support the steep, shake-shingled roofs. Unusual and so impressive; everybody seems drawn to them. Yet it is inside these buildings where you sense the true nature of the Iowa Lakeside Laboratory, present in the curious damp smells. Whiffs of rich prairie soil, wetland muck, dried plants, mothballs, ethanol, and formaldehyde, with top notes of coffee and stale cigar. It is in odors, as Faust knew, where memories reside. The smells in these old stone labs are the ghosts of their former inhabitants, and they convey the spirit of natural history practiced by these old-timers. It is the same spirit found at field stations around the world, dripping with the natural history facts, techniques, and perspectives that shape the foundation of the best of modern ecology. This spirit is found in the "-ology" subjects that form the backbone of field station curricula and ground the new discipline of conservation biology. Subjects that include mammalogy, ornithology, herpetology, ichthyology, invertebrate biology, parasitology, and algology—rarely taught nowadays on university campuses, or merely presented superficially; this, at a time when the world desperately needs such expertise.

It is the spirit of natural history that gives ecology its "older grace and intelligence" (Hawken 2007, 165). It is the portion of ecology that is grounded in facts and in inductive, bottom-up thinking. It permeates those who are curious; those with an "intelligent interest in the possibilities of living" (Meine 1988, 163). This spirit is present in the rubber-boot biologists working alone and with little fanfare at field stations and at other remote sites such as shacks, cabins, huts, wall tents, and trailers; places that put people close to nature without getting in its way. As I have noted in *Leopold's Shack and Ricketts's Lab* (Lannoo 2010, 156), this spirit is found after midnight, in the mist over a springtime wetland, with spring peepers calling nearby and crawfish frogs roaring in the distance. It is found in a couple of cold beers and a brisk, late night skinny-dip after a long hot day of studying prairie. It is there in an observation, in knowing that in the entire history of Earth and its humans, this is the first seeing. This spirit is deep in the student who, with ruler and notebook in hand and soaked to the skin in the middle of a driving spring squall, says, "I'd still rather be doing this than sitting in front of my computer." This spirit is more generally found in the ideas that question convention and move a discipline forward, not in ideologies that constrain and dictate. It arises spontaneously but not capriciously. This is the story of one place where, in 1909, the spirit appeared; this is the story of the Iowa Lakeside Laboratory.

The Iowa Lakeside Laboratory celebrated its centennial in 2009, and while there were plenty of festivities organized for this event, these were transient, and the idea arose to pull together a volume that would mark in some more permanent way this extraordinary milestone (the average life of field stations being something like sixteen years). But to do this book correctly, it has to be more than a remembrance. It is true that many of the most compelling images of the Lab come from the early Victorian days when students lived in tents and faculty wore neckties. But it also may be true that never in its entire history has Lakeside Lab been more relevant to science and to society at large than it is today.

Today we face a huge array of environmental problems including pollution, toxic waste, endocrine disruption, habitat loss, disease, invasive species, extinction, and climate change. The agricultural chemicals that disrupt reproduction in natural populations of wild animals have now been shown to do the same in humans. (Remember, Lakeside Lab is located in Iowa, the most intensively cultivated landscape on Earth, where less than one percent of presettlement vegetation remains.) Not only do we need laboratories in order to study these impacts (effects on nature being best examined in nature), and not only do we need laboratories with long histories to offer comparisons and insights into what we observe today, but we also need the kind of people that field stations produce—people who know nature and have learned how to think about nature. In the central Midwest, this place is the Iowa Lakeside Lab, situated in the remarkable community of Okoboji. While we reflect upon Lakeside's past, the true reason for the making of this book lies in the potential of this unique institution to produce the knowledge that infuses people with the spirit necessary to reshape humanity's future.

Toward this end I interweave the history of the Lakeside Laboratory with the people and ideas that helped shape this unusual institution. Using a chronological approach I describe the grounds and the buildings, and how they have changed throughout the years. I present the people and their ideas and describe how many of these original ideas persist today. I also explain how new ideas, born from experience, have grown the place. Finally, I suggest that the lessons learned at Lakeside can help shape a society that is more grounded, more sustainable, and richer in experiences and options. This may seem to be a leap, an idea bordering on the outrageous. But take a hard look around at this world we currently inhabit and ask yourself, "Isn't it time we tried something else?"

something heavy
in the midwestern air

. . . .

DURING THE LAST quarter or so of the nineteenth century, the upper Midwest produced some of the world's best naturalists cum ecologists. This was at the same time Thomas Macbride, Samuel Calvin, and Bohumil Shimek were conceiving the Iowa Lakeside Laboratory, and when Michigan's Douglas Lake and Minnesota's Itasca field stations were being built, and I think this was not an accident. There was something heavy in the air back then, something that powered an interest in studying the life sciences—the drive to understand something outside and larger than oneself. These tendencies may be lighter in the air today. As Aldo Leopold (1936, 181) pointed out in his obituary of Franklin Schmidt, while it was the first wave of North American pioneers who settled the land, it was the second wave of pioneers who were the scientists, studying the new (to the EuroAmerican eye) landscape and profoundly interested not only in the new species of plants and animals they found, but also in how these organisms fit together to produce the fertile midwestern ecosystems they were experiencing.

Among the earliest of these biologists was George Kruck Cherrie, born in Iowa in 1865. Cherrie graduated from Iowa State College and spent his career at the American Museum of Natural History. His specialty was the birds and mammals of Central and South America, which he helped to describe using specimens collected during his approximately forty expeditions. Cherrie is best known today for accompanying Theodore Roosevelt during his 1914 expedition down the River of Doubt.

Frederic Clements was born in Lincoln, Nebraska, in 1874. After faculty appointments at the universities of Nebraska and Minnesota, he moved to the Carnegie Institution in Washington, D.C., in 1917, where he remained until 1941. Clements worked at various research stations across the western United States and developed a theory of plant succession proposing that following a disturbance, plant communities change—generally from annual to perennial species—to eventually form climax communities appropriate to their environment. While severely criticized during his time, this idea has held and today Clements is revered as one of history's most influential ecologists.

Warder Clyde Allee was born on June 5, 1885, in Bloomington, Indiana. He received his undergraduate degree from Earlham College in 1908 and his Ph.D. from the University of Chicago in 1912. He returned to the University of Chicago in 1921, where his students included Ed Ricketts (see below) and Dick Bovbjerg (former director of Lakeside Lab and my first mentor). Aldo Leopold's oldest daughter Nina worked for Allee during World War II. Allee wrote a number of books, including *Animal Aggregations: A Study in General Sociology*, *Principles of Animal Ecology* (co-authored with Alfred E. Emerson, Orlando Park, Thomas Park, and Karl P. Schmidt), and *Cooperation among Animals, with Human Implications*. He is perhaps best known for describing what is now termed the Allee effect, which states that in animals per capita growth rate decreases as population size decreases, an important concept in conservation biology.

Rand Aldo Leopold, born January 11, 1887, in Burlington, Iowa, was the greatest field biologist of the first half of the twentieth century. After serving with the U.S. Forest Service in New Mexico, Leopold moved to Wisconsin where he began to act on his lifelong interest in wildlife. In 1933 he published *Game Management* and with it founded the discipline of wildlife biology. In 1935 he bought acreage and a shack in the Baraboo Hills region north of Madison. Weekends at the shack bought him time to think, his thinking became essays, and his essays became *A Sand County Almanac*, published a year after his tragic death fighting a prairie fire. Two decades after its publication, *Sand County* grew into a bible for the environmental movement—a must-read—and Leopold became lionized.

Olaus Johan Murie was born March 1, 1889, in Moorhead, Minnesota. After undergraduate training at North Dakota State University and Pacific University, Murie received his master's degree from the University of Michigan. In 1920 he joined the U.S. Biological Survey and spent the next six years in the field, with his half-brother Adoph, studying caribou life history and natural history. In 1924 he married Margaret (Mardy) Thomas. Olaus was always his own man, especially when it came to addressing federal policies designed to control predators. In 1937 Murie left the Biological Survey and became one of the leaders of the newly created

Wilderness Society. In 1954 he published his popular *Peterson Field Guide to Animal Tracks*. In 1956 he and Mardy began their successful campaign to convince President Eisenhower to designate the eight-million-acre Arctic National Wildlife Refuge. In addition to being a prolific writer, Murie was a gifted artist; the animals in his paintings appear to be breathing.

Ira Noel Gabrielson was born in Sioux Rapids, Iowa, on September 27, 1889. While attending Morningside College in Sioux City, he worked at Lakeside Lab; he graduated in 1912. Gabrielson then briefly taught biology at Marshall High School before joining the U.S. Biological Survey. For the next twenty years, he worked on a variety of wildlife management and research programs, mainly in the West. In 1935 he relocated to Washington, D.C., and became chief of the Survey's division of wildlife research. When in 1940 the Biological Survey and the Bureau of Fisheries were consolidated into the Fish and Wildlife Service, Gabrielson was made director, a position he held until after the war. In 1946 he retired and became president of the Wildlife Management Institute. In 1948 Gabrielson helped create the International Union for Conservation of Nature and Natural Resources (IUCN). For a time he was Rachel Carson's boss. In 1961 he helped organize the World Wildlife Fund and became its president.

Edward Flanders Robb Ricketts was born May 14, 1897, in Chicago, Illinois. Ricketts was educated at Illinois Normal and the University of Chicago. At Chicago he studied under, and was deeply influenced by, W. C. Allee (see above). In 1923 Ricketts moved to Monterey, California, and established Pacific Biological Laboratories, a biological supply company. Ricketts and his lab became the center of a lively artist group that included John and Carol Steinbeck, Joseph Campbell, John Cage, Henry Miller, and Bruce and Jean Ariss. In 1939 Ricketts published his landmark *Between Pacific Tides*, the first field guide to the intertidal invertebrates of the West Coast. In 1941 he collaborated with John Steinbeck on the classic ecological travelogue *Sea of Cortez*. In 1945 Steinbeck made "Doc" Ricketts the principal in his novella *Cannery Row*. Sadly, Ricketts died in 1948 after being struck by a train near the east end of Cannery Row.

Paul Lester Errington was born on June 14, 1902, in Bruce, South Dakota, and grew up among the wetlands of the vast Prairie Coteau. Following an undergraduate degree at South Dakota State Agricultural College (now, University), he did his graduate work in association with Aldo Leopold (see above). Errington received his doctorate in 1932 and became the head of Iowa State's newly established Fish and Wildlife Cooperative Unit, the first of its kind under a program conceived, and in part funded, by the Pulitzer Prize–winning cartoonist Ding Darling. Errington became the world's expert on wetland mammals and the broader topic of the role predation plays in controlling (or not) wildlife populations. Among Errington's many books are the classics *Of Men and Marshes, Muskrats and Marsh Management*, and *The Red Gods Call*.

Norman Fitzroy Maclean was born on December 23, 1902, in Clarinda, Iowa. Maclean's family moved to Montana when he was eight years old, but after attending Dartmouth, he returned to the Midwest when he joined the faculty of the University of Chicago, where he enjoyed a distinguished teaching career. Maclean and his family escaped Chicago to spend their summers at the family cabin on Seeley Lake in Montana. After Maclean's retirement in 1973, he wrote two classics of outdoor literature, *A River Runs through It* and *Young Men and Fire*. These works demonstrate Maclean's deep understanding of the relationships between humans and the natural world.

Taken together, Leopold's *Sand County Almanac*, Steinbeck and Ricketts's *Sea of Cortez*, and Maclean's *A River Runs through It* represent American literature's best attempt to explain the workings of humans through the workings of nature. And while it is these works that society sees, they are but a fraction—among the best of the best to be sure—of the work produced during a period of enormous effort and insight, when the midwestern United States was producing the best natural historians in the country, perhaps the world. And it is from this remarkable assemblage of talent that the Iowa Lakeside Laboratory emerged.

an opportunity
of magnificent possibilities

. . . .

IN 1909 when Thomas Huston Macbride founded the Iowa Lakeside Laboratory, the United States was on the brink of becoming great. Teddy Roosevelt had been in office eight years, and the country's image of itself as a nation cobbled from rugged individuals occupying a frontier landscape rested squarely on the broad shoulders of its bully president. This was a country that did not yet know who it was but was eager to find out. And one way it sought to know itself was to discover its nature, in the most literal sense. As the nineteenth century rolled into the twentieth, natural history surveys became institutionalized, great public museums were being built and stocked, and biological field stations were springing up along our coasts and at remote inland sites. In the Midwest, the University of Michigan's station at Douglas Lake and the University of Minnesota's station at Itasca were founded the same year as Iowa's Lakeside Lab.

But unlike the stations built by the public universities of Michigan and Minnesota, Iowa's Lakeside Laboratory began as a private enterprise. Macbride, who in 1914 became the president of the State University of Iowa (SUI), spent a great deal of time during the late 1890s in north-western Iowa studying the geology and flora of the region. He dreamed of a summer station to facilitate further discoveries and to "teach Iowans about Iowa" (Bovbjerg, Ulmer, and Downey 1974, 3). Then in the summer of 1908, he convinced some SUI alumni to purchase a five-acre tract on the western shore of West Lake Okoboji; the transaction was completed in January 1909. A large cottage was on site (and, newly restored, still is). A laboratory building was quickly built and the first session was held that summer. Ten courses were taught, which twenty-six students attended. Professors Thomas Macbride, Samuel Calvin, Bohumil Shimek, Robert Wylie, George Kay, and Bert Bailey—all dressed formally in coat and

. . . .

tie—were on the faculty. Fourteen public lectures were presented; lake steamers brought visitors on round trips. Students from fourteen Iowa colleges were charged $25 tuition and $4 per week room and board ("excellent tents, floor, walls and fly" [Bovbjerg, Ulmer, and Downey 1974, 4]). The newly constructed H-shaped laboratory (68 x 53 ft.) included three large and four small classrooms. When that first summer was over, Macbride ended his report with these remarks: "The alumni are face to face with an opportunity of magnificent possibilities, to the University at large and to this great commonwealth; but we have just begun. Permanent structures will some day crown the beautiful hilltop and pillars shine among its trees, and all visitors to our lakes, and all residents by the shores, and all lovers of nature in our State, will find from year to year refreshment and solace and joy in the halls and libraries of the Lakeside Laboratory, founded by the alumni of the University of Iowa" (Bovbjerg, Ulmer, and Downey 1974, 3).

The goal here is to tell the now century-old story of the Iowa Lakeside Laboratory. Personal accounts, photographs, and unpublished reports play a role in establishing the facts and presenting a sense of this amazing place. There is truth in this. But there is another Lakeside, the one that you can know only from being there and, once on site, to being open to all that it offers. In their classic collaboration *Sea of Cortez*, biologist Ed Ricketts and novelist John Steinbeck wrote (1941, 2):

> . . . the Mexican sierra has "XVII-15-IX" spines in the dorsal fin. These can be easily counted. But if the sierra strikes hard on the line so that our hands are burned, if the fish sounds and nearly escapes and finally comes in over the rail, his colors pulsing and his tail beating the air, a whole new relational externality has come into being—an entity which is more than the sum of the fish plus the fisherman. The only way to count the spines of the sierra unaffected by this second relational reality is to sit in a laboratory, open an evil-smelling jar, remove a stiff colorless fish from formalin solution, count the spines, and write the truth "D. XVII-15-IX." There you have recorded a reality which cannot be assailed—probably the least important reality concerning either the fish or yourself.

And so it is with the Iowa Lakeside Laboratory. You can read this book, stare at the pictures, even go there and "stroll around the grounds until you feel at home" (Simon 1967). But you will not really know Lakeside until you are in it, completely immersed in it. There you will find those old stone labs with their earthy natural history smells. Outside—somewhere, but maybe not nearby—you will find the professor and students muddy, sweaty, smelly, bug-bitten, scratched, and sunburned, but smiling—flush with the excitement of discovery. The professor: knowing but wanting the students to figure it out for themselves. The students: struggling, starting to see, beginning to get it, collectively and clumsily building toward some ecological truth that in two weeks will be second nature. And two weeks after that, leaving the place, fifty miles down the road, in the minds of the students the thought repeats itself over and over: "What just happened to me?" There is truth here also—perhaps the biggest truth to know about Lakeside, and almost certainly the source of the fierce loyalty that students and faculty share for the place. This truth—a form of lightning in a bottle—was there from the beginning. Recounting her experience as a student at Lakeside in 1910, Maud Brown wrote (1910, 13), "Little did I realize as I stepped ashore that I had reached a turning point in my life."

a brief history
of field stations

. . . .

BIOLOGICAL FIELD STATIONS are generally land-based operations with an infrastructure that supports teaching and/or research
programs. Field stations originated when professors realized they could
not authentically teach or research the biology of sea life from a classroom or laboratory hundreds of miles from the ocean. Many of the first
field stations were European and marine, situated on coasts. In the 1830s
a handful of Swedish naturalists established "an impromptu summer biological station" (Jack 1945, 9). A decade after, in 1843, Pierre-Joseph van
Beneden founded what is now considered the world's first true biological
station, the research-based Dune Laboratory in Ostend, Belgium. Later,
in 1859 the College of France at Concarneau established the Laboratory
of Marine Zoology and Physiology, which was also research oriented, on
the coast of Brittany. In 1873 Harvard's Louis Agassiz created the first
field station in North America, the Anderson School of Natural History
on Penikese Island off the coast of Massachusetts. At about the same time,
Anton Dohrn founded the prestigious Zoological Station of Naples.

The biological station idea spread swiftly and in many directions to
eventually embrace all habitats, not just coastal regions; field stations tend
to be located near or within unique habitats or in regions where biodiversity is high and easily accessible, although ships of exploration, such as
Darwin's *Beagle*, also have been considered field stations (Wyman, Wallensky, and Baine 2009, 584). By 1880 sixteen biological stations had been
established from Sweden and the Black Sea in Europe to Virginia and Illinois in the New World. By 1888 both the Marine Biological Laboratory
at Woods Hole, Massachusetts, and the Laboratory of the Marine Biological Association at Plymouth, England, were in operation. Between 1920
and 1930 alone, seventy new field stations were established (Jack 1945,

10). Today there are more than 1,300 field stations: over 300 in the United States and around 1,000 internationally (Moore 2010, 2).

Initial enthusiasm aside, field stations often fail. Prior to the Second World War, roughly ninety stations, or about one quarter of all stations established, had been abandoned—their average lifespan about sixteen years. The most common causes for failure have been the death of the director or founder (Louis Agassiz's death ended the Anderson School, although Woods Hole arose shortly thereafter), catastrophic fire (the Cornell University Biological Station), direct and indirect effects of war (the Royal Hungarian Marine Biological Station), funding cuts (the Biological Station of the United States Bureau of Fisheries at Woods Hole), personal disagreements over philosophy or control (the Mountain Laboratory of the University of Utah), even marine disasters (the wreckage of the *Pourquoi Pas?*) (Jack 1945, 11).

During the Second World War, field stations struggled. Young men and women who might have populated courses and research positions were overseas or in factories, and wartime budgets were bare-boned. Many stations failed.

Postwar participation in biological field stations varied. The surge in students supported by the GI Bill saw interest swell. Then in the mid 1950s the first flush of enthusiasm for the new field of molecular biology saw interest in organismal biology, and as a consequence interest in field stations, wane. Interest was rekindled in 1962 with the publication of Rachel Carson's *Silent Spring* and the birthing of the environmental movement. Field station enrollments again waned in the 1970s and have generally held steady or been declining since. Richard Bovbjerg's 1988 report on the status of Lakeside Lab commented on this enrollment decrease: "Across the land there has been a significant drop in registration at field stations. Some stations have gone under. The average registration drop over 10 years has been 40 percent. The same has been true at our station. This correlates with drops in graduate student numbers in the parent universities" (9). And despite the wide and varied nature of global environmental problems and the ability of field stations to address these problems, this is pretty much where we stand today (Whitesell, Lilieholm, and Sharik 2002, 13).

Knowing this, it is easy to become pessimistic because not only are field stations different places to study, they also produce a different type of student (Hodder 2009, 670). Undergraduate students on campus learn within a system. They are given books or website URLs and expected to fill their brains with the content of these sources. A lot of this happens at Lakeside also. But at Lakeside, students are encouraged to make their own observations and trust them over someone else's convention. Field station faculty show their students how to generate knowledge instead of absorbing it (Janovy and Major 2009, 218). Instruction at Lakeside becomes a variation of the old Chinese proverb: "Give a man a fish and you feed him for a day. Teach a man to fish and you feed him for a lifetime."

It is both discouraging and amazing how little today's university students know about natural history (Janovy and Major 2009, 218). Discouraging, because it wasn't always this way; Iowa doesn't produce farm kids like it used to, and even today's farm kids are plugged into their iPods and smart phones—it's difficult to hear frog calls wearing ear buds. But happily, it's amazing to see how quickly these same kids warm to the notion of nature, how easily they trade comfort and convenience for knowledge. At Lakeside, classes take field trips nearly every day, and at some point during every field trip students see something they have never seen before. More importantly, during these field trips they learn how to read nature. They learn why bur oaks are on east-facing slopes and not west, and why, when you stand on a high point in Okoboji and look east, all you see are trees, but when you turn around about all you see is grass. The instructors know that once patterns like these are pointed out, students naturally begin to look for other patterns, and with practice they learn to see them for themselves.

It is this ability to observe patterns and trust these observations that distinguishes Lakeside Lab and other field station alumni from campus alumni. Lakeside alumni often become big-picture people in a world occupied by specialists; they become society's glue. My host medical school is populated by specialists; there are few big-picture people, and therefore faculty and administrators seldom offer large-scale perspectives. As a result, expensive educational initiatives become more expensive as administrators deal with one unforeseen consequence after another. Places with similar problems could use the insights offered by field station alumni: these are kids who look at things differently—big picture, with confidence—and therefore become valuable colleagues.

the factors
of ecology are all here

* *

THOMAS MACBRIDE (1909, reprinted in Lannoo 1996, 27) wanted a field station where students could study nature in nature. For his site, he chose Okoboji—the lakes area of northwestern Iowa. Macbride knew what he was doing. Okoboji is edgy. From east to west, Okoboji marks a transition between ecoregions, from the eastern deciduous forest to the Great Plains. From north to south, Okoboji signals a shift from the recently glaciated landscape of the Minnesota lakes region to the much older and more dissected landscape of the Little Sioux Valley and ultimately the Missouri River Valley (Lannoo 1996, 11). Macbride's placement of his Lab meant students could study the components of most major midwestern ecosystems within an easy hike or horseback, buckboard, sailboat, or train ride from the Lab grounds.

As Debby Zieglowsky details (1985, 43), the origin of the Iowa Lakeside Laboratory was in, of all places, Hopkinton, Iowa, at the Lenox Collegiate Institution (prior to 1864 called Bowen Collegiate Institute, after 1884 called Lenox College; Lenox closed in 1944). In the early 1860s Samuel Calvin was on the faculty at Lenox and Thomas Macbride was his student. In 1874 Calvin moved to the State University of Iowa, where four years later Macbride joined him; together they constituted the Department of Natural Science. In those early days Macbride focused on botany, Calvin on geology and zoology. In 1890 a former student, Bohumil Shimek, joined Calvin and Macbride on the faculty. By the late 1890s this talented trio of naturalists had made several collecting trips to Okoboji and beyond to build their department's meager geologic, botanic, and natural history holdings. Travel in those days was slow; as they collected they conversed, and one of the things they discussed was building a field station for natural history research in the Okoboji area.

All three naturalists (ecology was at least a decade away from being

* *

recognized as a formal scientific discipline [Kohler 2006, 270]) recognized the uniqueness of the Okoboji landscape and therefore the distinctiveness of its plant and animal communities. As Macbride wrote in his 1909 report to the Iowa Academy of Science (reprinted in Lannoo 1996, 24–29):

In the first place the topography of Dickinson country is peculiar, unique. Situated on the western border of the Iowa Wisconsin drift, the region illustrates, as possibly no other equal area in the state, the special characteristics, not only of glacial moraines in general, but in particular the very expression of the Wisconsin moraine. In fact, I think that it must be admitted that the Okoboji lakes and their encompassing hills do indeed form the finest bit of morainic topography to be found on our western prairie.

Secondly, the region having Okoboji for its center is, by reason of the peculiar topography just mentioned, the field of a special floral display difficult to illustrate anywhere else within such narrow limits. We have a forest flora and a prairie flora; and neither in this part of the world has ever been adequately studied. It is believed that the fungal flora of the region, for instance, is especially rich and interesting. We have all kinds of habitat conditions, from aquatic to xerophytic. We have deep water, shallow water, but permanent; marshes, springs and [x]erophytic slopes and hill-tops, some so dry as to offer home to the vegetation of the higher western semi-arid plains. The plankton of the lakes is filled with desmids and diatoms and all manner of algal flora, during July and August rich beyond comparison in all that makes up the tide of life for these simple but fascinating forms.

For similar reasons, the fauna of the lake district will reward our constant study. The varied flora, just described, insures a varied fauna. The waters teem with animal life. Probably the protozoa of the whole valley will be found hiding on the vegetation of these [quiet] lakes and pools. Of course the avian and vertebrate aquatic fauna are rich, and even the terrestrial vertebrates are likely to prove more than commonly worthy of investigation. While this is writing the papers tell of a mountain lion shot in one of the nearby marshy lakes! It is not believed that carnivores of size are likely to abound, not to such extent at least to warrant a future visit by our nimrodic ex-president [Teddy Roosevelt; Macbride is referring to the Smithsonian-Theodore Roosevelt African Expedition, which at the time was receiving a great deal of publicity in the United States], but it is believed that natural science, in all its branches, entomology, ostracology, ornithology, will be greatly enriched by using such an opportunity for research as Okoboji may afford.

The terrestrial vegetation of early Okoboji, easily interpreted by the maps created by Shimek, was shaped by fire sweeping off the Great Plains (fig. 1). Pothole wetlands and lakes occurred as patches in a matrix of mixed-grass prairie. Rivers were largely treeless and described as prairie rivers. Trees were found only on the lee side of large lakes and wetland complexes or on steep, east-facing slopes. Most of these trees were fire-resistant bur oaks. In the 1859 surveyor's description of the west side of West Lake Okoboji, Charles A. M. Estes, deputy surveyor, described a "gently rolling" prairie with soils "1st rate." There were so few trees that individuals were noted: "A Cottonwood 20 inch s 73°e.70," "a Burr Oak 10 ins n 80°30'w 27." And where wetlands were encountered, entries such as "Enter Marsh nearly round. Leave same unfit for cult[ivation]" were written.

While Macbride believed that Okoboji was the perfect place to teach Iowans about the richness of their lakes, prairies, and forests, others had to be convinced, and Macbride's campaign to create his field station was arduous. As early as 1900 Macbride urged: "Naturalists will find here exceptional advantages for the prosecution of their work, and summer schools of science might here flourish as in no other quarter of the state" (Zieglowsky 1985, 45).

Despite his enthusiasm, Macbride understood that establishing a field station in this remote area was going to be logistically difficult. One of the many factors hampering his efforts was a technicality—a provision in the state constitution prohibiting the formation of any "branch" of the university in any place other than Iowa City. When in 1908 the five-acre E. B. Smith tract became available on West Lake Okoboji, Macbride approached the members of the University of Iowa Alumni Association about purchasing the property. The site, Macbride knew, could be privately owned by the Alumni Association and offered to the university's science departments for fieldwork. The group agreed and began fund-raising by offering stock in the venture. Shares in the Iowa Lakeside Lab-

---

1. Bohumil Shimek's 1920 map of Dickinson County, Iowa. Note the high concentrations of pre-swampbusting era wetlands indicated to the west of Lakeside Lab (left center) and along the Burlington, Cedar Rapids, and Northern Railroad tracks (the old Duck Railroad) from Milford north to Okoboji. These wetland densities reflect their abundance throughout the region. Note also the presence of Sylvan, Pratt, and Pillsbury lakes in the southwestern corner of the county. This huge wetland complex has since been drained for agriculture, although evidence of these basins, their shorelines, and their animals remains today. Courtesy of University Archives, Department of Special Collections, University of Iowa Libraries.

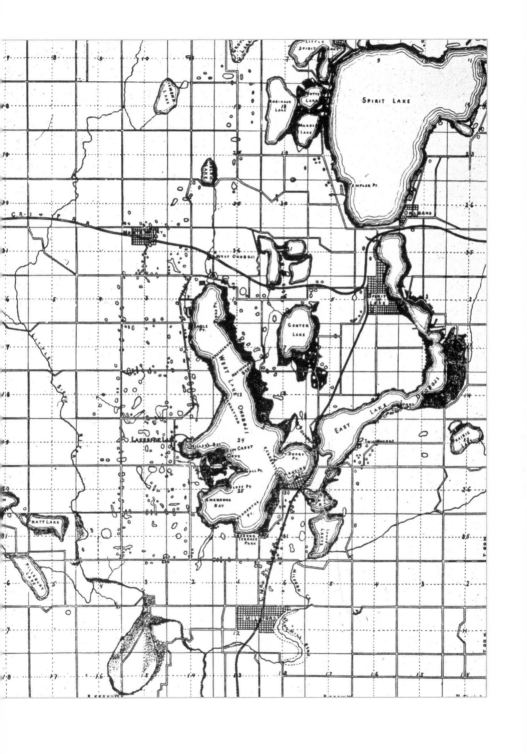

oratory Association were offered at $10 each; initially only alumni were allowed to invest (fig. 2). By January 1909 $6,500 had been raised and the property purchased through an intermediary, W. L. Hinds.

Situated along the west-central side of West Lake Okoboji, on Little Miller's Bay, the site contained 500 feet of partially wooded shoreline steeply rising to a hill, a "well-built eight-room cottage, a two-room cottage, an icehouse or boathouse, an electric-light plant, and a water pumping station" (Zieglowsky 1985, 46). The large cottage was known as Unalaklick (sometimes spelled Unalakleek), and the purchase agreement included one gasoline launch (also named *Unalaklick*), one sailboat (*South Breeze*, which Hinds kept, perhaps as payment for his services), one rowboat with a gasoline engine attachment, and all tools stored in the power house and the gasoline storage house (fig. 3).

2. Thomas Macbride's stock certificate (number 108) representing shares in the Iowa Lakeside Laboratory. Shares were offered in 1909 and were worth $10 apiece; this certificate is for thirty-five shares. Courtesy of University Archives, Department of Special Collections, University of Iowa Libraries.

3. Students lounging in front of Main Cottage during the Lab's earliest years. Note the presence of rain barrels under the downspouts and the laboratory building in the background. Courtesy of University Archives, Department of Special Collections, University of Iowa Libraries.

In addition, the Alumni Association raised $1,000 for the construction of a laboratory building. Plans were drawn to include a lecture hall designed to seat 125, classrooms, faculty offices, and a library. The building had electric lighting, electrically heated water baths, running water, tanks, sinks, and all necessary laboratory furniture. The building was constructed in Iowa City, shipped to Okoboji, and assembled on site.

Later that summer Macbride would write (1909, reprinted in part 1985, 67), "the factors of ecology and distribution are all here, in large part so far, unexplored and certain to interest for centuries generation after generation of Iowa students."

the iowa lakeside laboratory as a student sees it

BY MAUD BROWN, 1910

· ·

OKOBOJI—"PLACE OF REST." What! A school? The best school ever conducted was held beneath the plane trees where the students walked and talked with the master. Are not the Iowa oaks as picturesque as the sycamores of Athens? And, you alumni, would you give a walk through the deep woods with Macbride or a tramp over the morainic knobs with Calvin for discourse with your heathen philosopher?

"We wish to go to the Lakeside Laboratory," we announced impressively to the pilot of the little double-deck steamer at the pier.

"The other boat, ma'am. Here," he called across, "these folks want to go to the bug-house." We walked aboard the little "Queen" just as she in a most unfeminine voice announced her departure, and we rocked out over the water counted rough that morning as a stiff breeze from the north whipped the tops of the white caps. North and south stretched seven miles of water, while a mile and a half away, east and west, the banks rose in wooded slopes.

"I wonder what sort of aquatic creatures those are!" I remarked tentatively to the pilot as he punched a little pink slip and returned it to me. "They seem rather active for whales."

He looked up the bay. "Oh, motor boat races have started. We'll get a good view. The big one's gaining—there—it's passed them!" And in less time than we are using in the telling, the thing passed in a cloud of spray. Two smaller boats trailed behind, and several more followed in the distance.

"Pretty good clip for the water. Look up to the north end there—sail boat race is on."

I looked and saw a dozen graceful sail boats dipping and turning, forming in a line for the start, but the pudgy Queen churned her way steadily westward and our view of the race was cut off by the long red-roofed Manhattan that crouched at the bend of the lake.

We soon entered "Miller's Bay." Ahead of us, topping one of the less densely wooded knolls, appeared the low gray and white buildings of the laboratory. The deep woods along the lake, the prairies stretching off beyond, and the wealth of aquatic plant life through which the Queen now chugged disgustedly, gave the promise of material enough to quicken the pulse of any student of nature, whether that pulse respond to heartbeats ecological, ornithological, entomological, or geologic.

As we neared the pier, a fisherman on the sandbar held up an armlong pickerel shining in the sun. A boatman was carefully picking over masses of green stuff which he was bringing up from the bottom and was handling as a miser caresses hid gold pieces. Little did I realize as I stepped ashore that I had reached a turning point in my life. That, whereas formerly all unfamiliar green growth, whether on land or in the water, had been dubbed collectively as "moss," I was destined to return to my home prating glibly of *Ceratophyllum*, *Myriophyllum* and *Pleurococcus*.

A tall young man who had been gyrating along the surface of the earth at the end of a butterfly net came up and escorted me to the cottage, explaining that, this being Saturday morning, the students were scattered on field work along the lines of their special interests.

He introduced me to the kindly housekeeper, who invited me to rest on the broad, screened-in porch which ran along two sides of the cottage in which were contained the living rooms of the station. She pointed out to me the row of tents at the crest of the hill and explained that these accommodated the men students, while down the path and past the spring was the farm house where the women lived. The laboratory, a low H-shaped structure, stood to the north, and a small cottage behind.

Under a tree lay two high-school boys from a nearby cottage, being tutored in mathematics by an ambitious young man who was paying his own expenses through college.

Soon groups began to return. A half dozen ornithologists with bird glasses swinging over their shoulders were enthusiastic over the newly found nest of young bitterns. Another group laden with baskets talked learnedly of agarics and slime molds, while down the hill came a lone enthusiast boasting of twelve species of grasses from High Point.

All gathered on the porch for a few minutes' rest before going on for lunch, and later, while waiting for the mail.

A trim little launch, the "Old Gold," floating an "Iowa" pennant, came up and carried the geology class away to study the natural rip-rapping along the shores, which I went in and duly matriculated as a student in that most delightful school, the Okoboji Lakeside Laboratory, established by the alumni of the State University of Iowa.

The next day being Sunday, we gathered for religious services in the laboratory room, the sermon being the usual, from one of the representative preachers or teachers of the state. After dinner, at which the speaker was the guest of honor, the day was passed quietly, many students gathering about the big library table writing home.

On Monday, the real work began. Classes in the various sciences occupied the morning; classes and fieldwork, the afternoon. Often the classwork was entirely out-of-doors, the students grouped informally about some object of interest.

About four-thirty, all took the daily dip into the lake and swimming lessons were generously given by those of natatorial accomplishments.

The evenings were variously spent: the collectors over their pins, cyanide bottles and plant presses; the bookish, over their study tables; the musical, around the farmhouse piano; and some of the undergraduates using the glorious moonlight nights as God intended them to be used. Often the whole family went for a sail after supper, and the indescribable glory of the sunset waters is something that will not easily be forgotten.

Two nights a week, the best talent of the university was drawn upon for illustrated lectures on scientific subjects. These lectures, as also the Sunday services, seemed to fill a long-felt want among the cottages who attended in weekly increasing numbers.

Altogether, when the all-too-short weeks were over, they were voted entirely profitable: by the high school teacher and college professor as they nailed up excelsior-stuffed crates of material for winter's use; by the undergraduate with some well-earned "credits"; by the special student, hugging a few more facts developed in the summer's study of his hobby; and by the plain citizen who has learned to love outdoors more through the new wonders revealed. As they once more step aboard the little steamer, there is an intangible something about them that speaks of health—not only of renewed bodily vigor, but of something down deep in their natures that has been renewed and refreshed, and from which life-giving currents will flow throughout the year. So that the teacher will bring truth nearer to the hearts of men, the investigator will see with keener insight, and the citizen will love God and man the better.

the victorians

1909–1932

SOON AFTER W. L. Hinds purchased the E. B. Smith acreage on January 11, 1909, the State University of Iowa (SUI, later the University of Iowa) printed and distributed first a preliminary announcement (fig. 4) describing the formation of the laboratory and its mission. A short while later, the university published a more detailed bulletin that included the curriculum (fig. 5). Two sessions were offered, beginning in June 1909. The first was six weeks long, the second four. Macbride taught mycology, Calvin offered Iowa physiography, Shimek covered field ecology and plant taxonomy (fig. 6). Two other SUI professors were on the faculty: Robert B. Wylie taught aquatic plant biology and plant physiology; George F. Kay offered elementary mineralogy and petrology. Bert H. Bailey, from Coe College, taught general and advanced zoology as well as ornithology. Invitations were sent to students from all recognized state colleges and universities, and the State Board of Education (renamed the State Board of Regents in 1954) offered scholarships. Students arrived from SUI, Iowa State College, Buena Vista College, Coe College, Cornell College, Drake University, Highland Park College, Iowa Wesleyan University, Lenox College, Morningside College, Parsons College, Simpson Centenary, Tabor College, and Upper Iowa University. Women and men attended in nearly equal numbers (fig. 7).

Students generally arrived by train. The Milwaukee line—the north-south track from Des Moines (also known as the Duck Railroad)— dropped off students in Arnold's Park (see Maud Brown's account). The Rock Island line—running east-west—deposited students in West Okoboji (at that time situated at the north end of West Lake Okoboji, not at the south end, where a town bearing the same name is now located). These railroads and towns are clearly marked on Shimek's map (see fig. 1). Lake steamboats ferried students to the Lakeside dock (fig. 8), while their luggage came overland in a buckboard.

4. A pocket-sized pamphlet printed in the late winter/early spring of 1909 announcing the intention to offer instruction at the Iowa Lakeside Laboratory. Courtesy of University Archives, Department of Special Collections, University of Iowa Libraries.

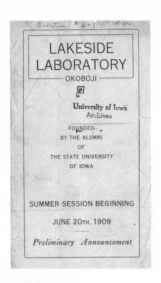

5. The full bulletin printed during the spring of 1909 describing the nature and program of instruction at the Iowa Lakeside Laboratory during its first season of operation. Courtesy of University Archives, Department of Special Collections, University of Iowa Libraries.

6. Arrival of Thomas Macbride, Samuel Calvin, and Robert Wylie at the Iowa Lakeside Laboratory dock in 1909. Courtesy of University Archives, Department of Special Collections, University of Iowa Libraries.

7. Thomas Macbride (center) and the proud students, instructors, staff, and associates in attendance during the Iowa Lakeside Lab's first season (1909). Courtesy of University Archives, Department of Special Collections, University of Iowa Libraries.

8. The steamboat *Queen* ferrying students to the Lakeside dock during the Lab's earliest years. Courtesy of University Archives, Department of Special Collections, University of Iowa Libraries.

As Maud Brown describes (1910, 12), students checked in at Main Cottage, where they were assigned housing. Most students lived in tents. The 1912 summer bulletin described this lodging: "A tent is provided with a wooden floor and covered with a fly, and contains individual cots with mattresses, a pail, wash basin, and chairs. Students will bring their own bedding, towels, and soap" (Zieglowsky 1985, 48). Students also had the option of boarding at a local hotel or with nearby farm families. In 1910 Maud Brown suggested that while the men slept in tents, the women bunked in a farmhouse off the lab grounds to the immediate south. Photos from a few years later show that women also lived in tents. During these early years students were expected to help carry water, weed the vegetable garden, and cut firewood.

Students conducting advanced research were expected to bring their own supplies: "Boxes, bottles, and preserving fluids for the care of such materials, and paper for plant presses are especially in demand. Mason fruit-jars may be purchased at the local stores, but other supplies of this kind should be brought by the students who expect to use them" (Zieglowsky 1985, 48).

Some traditions established in those early days persist. Perhaps the most important is that hard work be offset by hard play. "It is the purpose of the Station to offer opportunities for serious work to students and lovers of Nature. Five days of the week will be given to field excursions. While mere pleasure will not be permitted to encroach upon the serious work of the Station, abundant opportunities will be offered after working hours for recreation, such as swimming, boating, etc. Instruction in swimming will be given to those who desire it. Row-boats for private use may be hired at the Hotel" (Zieglowsky 1985, 49) (fig. 9).

9. During Lakeside's earliest years, an afternoon swimming party off what is now called the Presby beach. Note in the near background the Lakeside boathouse and launch, and in the far background the nearly treeless expanse of prairie and wetland that would, after 1931, become the property of the Station. Courtesy of the State Historical Society of Iowa, Iowa City.

The 1909 summer bulletin offers an example of how Macbride, Calvin, and Shimek envisioned instruction in field studies at the Iowa Lakeside Lab.

A. FIRST TERM—JUNE 21—JULY 31

BOTANY

1. Mycology   5 hours

A study in laboratory and field of local fungal flora. Open to a limited number of students. Professor Macbride

2. Biology of Aquatic Plants   5 hours

A general course on the structure and life-history of fresh-water plants. Morphology considered in relation to function and the factors of environment. The study will include both the lower and higher orders, but with special emphasis on the Algae. Professor Wylie

3. The Nature of Plants   5 hours

Dealing with the structure and organization of higher plants. A course designed to supplement elementary considerations and to afford a view-point in the teaching and study of Botany. Professor Wylie

4. Research in Botany

Special individual work for advanced students. Credit according to work accomplished. Professors Macbride and Wylie

GEOLOGY

1. The Physiography of Iowa   2 ½ hours

The surface features of Iowa, together with the agencies and processes which have been instrumental in their development, will be discussed in the course of daily lectures beginning June 21, and continuing three weeks. The physiographic characters of any locality depend on a complex of causes, dynamic agents as the atmosphere, water, and glacial ice. These subjects and their relation to the genesis of the topographic forms found in our own state will be presented as fully as time will permit.

Saturday of each week will be devoted to field work in connection with this course. Weather permitting three excursions will be taken for the study of glacial phenomena in which this region abounds. Professor Calvin

2. Elementary Mineralogy and Petrology   2 ½ hours

This course is intended to familiarize the student with the common minerals and rocks and the methods by which they are identified. In the laboratory, the physical characters of the common rock-making minerals and of the ores of iron, copper, lead, zinc, etc., will be studied; in the field, collections of the common rocks will be made and the origin and classification of the rocks discussed. Professor Kay

3. Research in Geology

Graduate students with requisite preparation may in so far as possible be assigned definite research studies to be carried on in the field. Professors Calvin and Kay

ZOOLOGY

1. General Zoology   5 hours

This course is planned for those who desire elementary work in zoology. It will include the study of the available type forms of both vertebrates and invertebrates, and will consist of lectures, laboratory, and field work. Aquatic forms will be given special attention. Professor Bailey

2. Advanced Zoology   5 hours

Graduate students, and those who have already familiarized themselves with type forms, will find here the opportunity to investigate more critically some one species or group with a view to becoming better acquainted with the life histories and morphology of aquatic and terrestrial forms. Professor Bailey

3. Ornithology   Hours as arranged

The lake region of Iowa offers a most interesting and delightful field for the study of avian fauna. A course will be offered consisting of field work and lectures that will deal with the ancestry of our modern birds, their life histories, and the adaptation of parts to environment. Student should be provided with field or opera glasses. Professor Bailey

B. SECOND TERM, AUGUST 2–AUGUST 28

1. Field Ecology   5 hours

A field and laboratory study of the flora of Lake Okoboji and vicinity with special reference to the influence of environment as exhibited in distribution, and in physiological and structural adaptations. This is practically a continuation of Course II, but may not be taken independently, and is designed primarily for teachers of botany in secondary schools, but will be of assistance to those who are interested in real nature study. Professor Shimek

2. Plant Taxonomy   5 hours

A course designed to acquaint the student with the methods of identification and classification of plants, and the use of the more common reference books for this purpose. A field and laboratory course which supplements Course 1, but may be taken independently, and without previous preparation in botany. Professor Shimek

Note—Illustrated lectures are given in connection with courses 1 and 2.

3. Research Work

Facilities for research work will be provided, especially along ecological and taxonomic lines. Professor Shimek

---

When not in class, faculty engaged in their own research and encouraged advanced students to participate. Much of this research was descriptive, centered on the identification and taxonomic descriptions of the native plants and animals encountered, although ecological relationships were also emphasized. During the first decade of the Lab, nearly fifty papers were published in journals such as *Science*, the *Wilson Bulletin*, the *Botanical Gazette*, and the *Proceedings of the Iowa Academy of Science* (Zieglowsky-Baker 1990, 190–99). Research topics included descriptions of the geology, ecosystems, and plants and animals of the region; censuses of prairies, forests, and lakes; and physical science studies on lake dynamics and evaporative water loss. The faculty also penned essays on topics such as geology and revelation, as well as conservation (Zieglowsky-Baker 1990, 190–99).

Change was inevitable, especially among the older faculty. Calvin died in 1911. Macbride served as the director during the first three summers and again in 1913. By 1914 he was the president of the State University of Iowa. But the new administrative responsibilities taxed his time and his health, and in 1916, at age 68, Macbride retired and moved to Seattle. Shimek took over the directorship of Lakeside in 1912 (fig. 10) and T. C. Stephens in 1914. Between 1915 and 1918 R. B. Wylie and Shimek directed the Lab in alternate years.

Although conditions were rustic and space was cramped, Lakeside's first ten years were idyllic times. About thirty students attended each summer, and both teaching and research were conducted at high levels (fig. 11). The First World War changed this. In 1918 men accepted for

10. There were giants on the earth in those days: Lakeside Lab faculty in 1921. From left to right, Charles R. Keyes, founder of the Iowa Archeological Society; Bohumil Shimek, one of Lakeside's founders; Louis H. Pammel, botanist from Iowa State University; George F. Kay, geologist from the University of Iowa; and T. C. Stephens, ornithologist from Morningside College. Courtesy of University Archives, Department of Special Collections, University of Iowa Libraries.

summer positions at the Station received their draft notices a week before the first session was to begin. Only twelve students attended.

The war effort was all consuming. In May 1918 Macbride wrote Shimek: "There is but one thing now for all of us to consider; How may this war be won and the world delivered?" (Zieglowsky 1985, 51). Shimek saw the war as an opportunity for his homeland, Czechoslovakia, to become freed from Austrian rule. He raised $100,000 in Iowa alone to support the resistance army. Macbride wrote, "I rejoice in what you are doing: you will smile when I tell you that I am 'on the reserve list'" (Zieglowsky 1985, 51).

Yet, Shimek agonized about the fate of the Lab. Despite his own anxieties, Macbride tried to ease Shimek's mind: "Do not let anything prevent your most praiseworthy efforts to keep our people up to the proper spirit in winning this war. We've got to win it, and I am rejoicing in you as a son" (Zieglowsky 1985, 51).

11. During Lakeside's earliest years, class field trip to High Point, located a few hundred yards directly west of the Lab grounds. Note the absence of trees on the landscape; native prairie plants remain on this slope today. In the late 1920s the University of Iowa Alumni Association unsuccessfully attempted to buy this property and the wetland behind, to the west. At the time this photo was taken, High Point was private property, owned by James A. Beck. Courtesy of the State Historical Society of Iowa, Iowa City.

Macbride's concerns about the Lab centered on funding. At this time, support for Lakeside came entirely from the sale of Lakeside Lab Association stock and from private donations (especially Macbride's). Raising money for faculty salaries, upkeep of the grounds and buildings, and providing and maintaining research equipment was proving difficult, even with Macbride's generous assistance. The trustees of the Lakeside Laboratory Association met in Iowa City to discuss the situation, and Macbride wrote in a follow-up letter to SUI President Walter A. Jessup:

> At a meeting of the trustees of the Lakeside Laboratory, held at the [SUI] President's office on the evening of November 10th, 1918, and to which University professors were invited for conference, deans Seashore and Kay, and professors Shimek, Wylie, Stromsten and Macbride being present, the whole laboratory situation was carefully and thoroughly discussed. It was the sense of

those present that the time had arrived when the laboratory should be placed on more permanent footing and it was agreed that it should be made a purely research station under the direction of the University Graduate College.

After the conference, the following resolution by Kuehnle, trustees Sanders, Kuehnle and Macbride being present, was unanimously adopted: Resolved that it is the sense of the Board of Trustees of the Macbride Lakeside Laboratory that the [use of the] property be tendered to the State University of Iowa for scientific research on such terms as shall be mutually satisfactory. (Bovbjerg, Ulmer, and Downey 1974, a-29)

The immediate financial crisis was over. In exchange for assuming responsibility for covering faculty salaries and purchasing equipment, Lakeside Lab was to become a pure research institution (as opposed to a teaching and research venture) under control of the SUI Graduate College. Classes were suspended, and for the next decade, the Lab staff was limited to two SUI professors and their advanced research students. Between 1919 and 1927 Robert Wylie and Frank Stromsten directed the Station, generally in alternate years. George W. Martin assumed control from 1928 to 1933 (Bovbjerg, Ulmer, and Downey 1974, a-4).

The Lakeside Bulletin of 1919 reads:

Announcement of the
IOWA LAKESIDE LABORATORY
Summer of 1919
JUNE 23—AUGUST 30

Beginning with the summer session of 1919 the laboratory will be placed exclusively on a research basis and the session will be lengthened to ten weeks.

The Laboratory will be open to investigators from June 23 to August 30. Man may be accommodated with quarters a few days earlier than the opening date, but the Station Mess will not be open until Saturday, June 21.

For the summer of 1919 provision will be made for independent workers only, and the Laboratory will be organized on a research basis. Experienced research workers, students engaged on theses, and advanced graduate or undergraduate students who are prepared to undertake investigation are invited to the privileges of the Laboratory.

Professor Robert Bradford Wylie of the Department of Botany and professor Frank A. Stromsten of the Department of Zoology representing the University of Iowa, will be in residence during the summer and will offer to investigators any service they may be able to render.

Admission to the Laboratory is arranged only through the Director. Correspondence should be opened in advance. There will be no tuition or Station fee for those admitted. Dormitory facilities and tents, as now available, are offered to investigators without charge. The Station Mess provides board at moderate costs on a cooperative basis.

Members of the Laboratory should bring their own microscopes, special apparatus, containers, reagents, etc. Cots and mattresses are furnished but no bedding is provided. A list of suggested items of personal equipment may be obtained from the Director upon request.

Correspondence should be addressed to,

> Professor Robert Bradford Wylie
> Director Lakeside Laboratory
> Iowa City, Iowa
> (Address after June 15, Milford, Iowa)

The Roaring Twenties were not so roaring for the Station. As Zieglowsky writes (1985, 54): "Reports from the station directors were filled with pleas for repair of the station buildings: 'the main cottage needs a new roof'; 'the porch will soon require repair'; 'the laboratory building needs a number of new windows'; 'all the buildings in need of paint.'" The Iowa Lakeside Laboratory Association initiated a campaign to raise a $10,000 endowment. The results were disappointing; after two years, they had not come close to their goal, although the money that had been raised provided a source of funding for emergency repairs and nominal upkeep.

The increasingly shoddy appearance of the buildings and the overall decrepit look of the place deeply concerned Macbride, and in a 1928 letter to director Martin, he offered his assistance: "I wish you would advise me if there is any particular attention that might be given to the buildings or approaches or grounds that would make the property seem less neglected. I understand that nothing has been done toward keeping it up for some time. I do not think it should be permitted to present such an unsightly appearance, so long as we are associating it with the university work. I will look after the matter if you tell me just what is needed, and will act promptly" (Zieglowsky 1985, 55).

The condition of the grounds notwithstanding, during the 1920s, research at the Lab was booming. In 1920 the famous University of Wisconsin limnological team of Edward Birge and Chauncy Juday published their assessment of West Lake Okoboji. Frank Blanchard from the University of Michigan spent a portion of 1920 studying the amphibians and reptiles of the Okoboji region. Other research included additional floral and faunal surveys, morphological and life history studies of plants and animals, studies of vertebrate physiology and developmental biology, behavioral studies, food habits studies, and work on pollination biology (Zieglowsky-Baker 1990, 190–99).

In 1929 courses were again offered, producing a curriculum that once more combined instruction with research. Director Martin wrote, "we are trying the experiment of reverting to the plan [of teaching and research] which was so markedly successful as administered by President Macbride in the earlier days" (Zieglowsky 1985, 55).

The course offerings of 1929 and 1930 appeared as follows:

1929

Botany 5L Systematic Botany   5 cr.
    June 10 to July 13. Identification and classification of vascular
    plants, with emphasis on the prairie flora. Professor Shimek.

Botany 126L Microscopy of Water   5 cr.
    July 15 to August 16. Water sources; pollution problems;
    taxonomic survey of aquatic organisms. Associate Professor
    Martin, Miss Gilmore.

Botany 225 (226)L Research (Mycology)   ar.
    Associate Professor Martin.

Zoology 201 (202)L Comparative Physiology (Research)   ar.
    Assistant Professor Helff.

1930

FIRST TERM (JUNE 16–JULY 19)

Botany 1L Field Botany   5 cr.
    General ecology and taxonomy of plants including field
    study of all the principle groups. Autecology. Mr. Conard.

Zoology 1L Field Zoology   5 cr.
    Identification of native animals, with special reference to

vertebrates, their life histories, habits and relation to environment. (Field glasses, for bird study, will be needed.)
Dr. Wright.

SECOND TERM (JULY 21–AUGUST 23)

Botany 2L Field Botany   5 cr.
Taxonomy and ecology of vascular plants with special reference to prairie and forest. Synecology. Mr. Kelley.

Zoology 2L Field Zoology   5 cr.
A continuation of 1L with special reference to invertebrates.
Dr. Wright.

During both terms advanced work and research in systematic botany, mycology, and animal and plant ecology, as arranged.
STAFF.

An increasing problem was space. Okoboji's reputation as a resort and vacation destination was resulting in the development of its shorelines and associated uplands. Land was becoming less agricultural and more suburban. The early ability of students to collect beyond the boundaries of the lab grounds (see fig. 11) must have been curtailed as people began building and living on the land, and the original five acres must have seemed cramped for professors trying to run concurrent classes with dozens of students.

The solution became expansion, and the early concerns about fundraising for routine building and equipment maintenance became concerns about fund-raising to build a larger Station. Macbride knew Lakeside's future hinged on the acquisition of more property both for building infrastructure (there was an immediate need for more permanent housing) and for field exploration and experimentation. When raising money proved frustrating, he confided to Shimek, "Okoboji worries me nights" (Zieglowsky 1985, 52).

Several options for expansion were considered, including the acquisition of the property directly west, across the road, that incorporated High Point and a large wetland (fig. 12). This transaction could not be arranged (but wouldn't that have been something). Finally in 1928 several tracts of land on Little Miller's Bay to the north of the Station became available. The first Myerly tract, jointly owned by Jennie C. Myerly and her husband J. I. Myerly, and Anna Frye and her husband J. S. Frye, consisted of twelve acres along the north shore and was sold to the Lakeside Laboratory Association for $2,000 on June 17, 1929 (Zieglowsky 1985, 55). In 1931 the Myerlys sold a second lakeshore lot to the Lab (Bovbjerg, Ulmer, and Downey 1974, a-39–40).

Acquiring the seventy-two-acre Floete property presented a greater challenge. Franklin Floete drove a hard bargain, asking a suburban price ($15,000) for what Macbride felt was agricultural property. Macbride wrote to Shimek:

> Let Mr. Floete know that we folk are not realtors, speculators, buying land for subdivision, simply to sell again at an extravagant [sic] profit, nor indeed at all; we spend freely asking no return for the sake of the intellectual life of men, for the uplift of men in all clearness and cleaness of thinking. He can, I believe, realize the value of such attainment against which money does not count. (Zieglowsky 1985, 55–56)

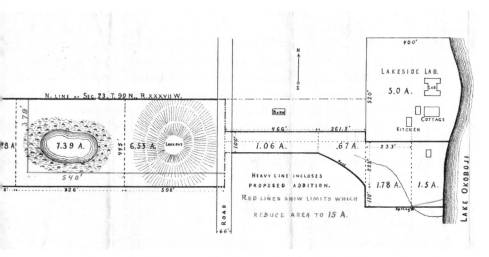

12. One early expansion plan, never realized, was to buy High Point (Lookout on the map) and the wetland to the west, with a narrow (100') corridor in between. One important consideration appears to have been to keep the purchase to fifteen acres, probably for financial reasons. Had this property been bought, the Lakeside grounds would have been hourglass shaped. The properties to the east of the road (running vertically, north/south, through the center of the diagram; 1.06, 0.67, 1.78, and 1.5 acres) were purchased. Courtesy of University Archives, Department of Special Collections, University of Iowa Libraries.

He vented a similar frustration to Stromsten:

Now Mr. Floete has the land we want, not as farm-land but as small town-lots for sale, I believe! I had never heard that the whole country is platted—: a town, if you please; and it is intended that city prices shall obtain. So Mr. Floete proposes to sell us land worth 3 or $4000, at present market prices, for $14,000, city lot prices, I presume! (Zieglowsky 1985, 56)

Macbride and Shimek were not the sort of men who backed away from a challenge. The Floete property was essential if Lakeside Lab was to survive, so Shimek put his wartime fund-raising experiences to work and sought donations. He made speaking appearances at SUI alumni gatherings throughout the state, encouraging members to contribute. And they did. Some donors had no interest in Lakeside itself but donated to acknowledge Macbride. Larger donations also arrived. The largest, $5,000, came from Macbride himself. As fund-raising continued and money came in, the Lakeside Laboratory Association began seriously negotiating with Floete. They persuaded him to lower his asking price in return for a large down payment and payment in full within a year. Finally, on April 8, 1929, Shimek sent Macbride a telegram:

CONTRACT SIGNED AND SIX THOUSAND FOUR HUNDRED DOLLARS PAID DOWN. FIFTEEN HUNDRED MORE PROMISED DEFINITELY AND MORE IN SIGHT. GO TO DES MOINES WEDNESDAY. DAVENPORT WILL DO SOMETHING. ALSO CEDAR RAPIDS. WE HAVE TAKEN OVER INSURANCE ON BUILDINGS AMOUNTING TO FOUR THOUSAND DOLLARS. POSSESSION GIVEN IMMEDIATELY. (Zieglowsky 1985, 64)

With these two acquisitions, and the purchase of the second Myerly tract by the end of 1931, Lakeside Lab had expanded to about ninety-five acres and the Station was beginning to assume its modern proportions (figs. 13A, B). Lakeside had returned to the founder's initial vision as a teaching

---

13. Two versions of the same map demonstrating the dynamic thinking about Lakeside expansion in 1929. An early draft (A), containing the former landowner names (Floete and Myerly), included the expansion plans across the road depicted in 17. The second (B) was published in the 1930 bulletin (produced in August 1929) and included the south five acres, the two Floete properties (thirty-two and forty acres), and the Myerly property (twelve acres), exclusive of a small lakeshore lot that appears to have been sold to the Lab in 1931. Courtesy of University Archives, Department of Special Collections, University of Iowa Libraries.

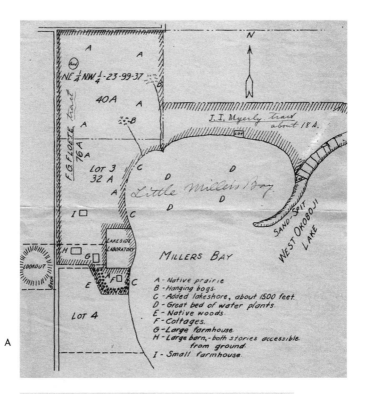

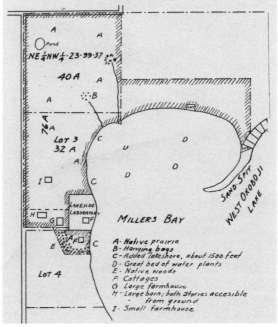

A

B

and research institution, with research guiding teaching. Descriptive biology, including plant and animal morphology and taxonomy—the chief biological interests of the day—predominated, but ecological relationships were also stressed. Lakes were central to these studies. Stromsten studied limnology; Wylie studied the aquatic vascular plants (macrophytes); L. H. Tiffany, G. W. Prescott, and G. Smith studied the freshwater algae and became internationally known. Shimek pursued his broad interests in Pleistocene stratigraphy, prairies, and mollusks. Martin studied fungi (mycology).

As former director Richard Bovbjerg emphasized in his 1974 report, the major feat of the first two decades was survival (Bovbjerg, Ulmer, and Downey 1974, 6). But by showcasing a talented faculty, Lakeside had established itself as an important field station and, with the 1929 and 1931 acquisitions, possessed the land necessary to secure its future.

hard times and stone labs

* *

IN 1932 with the founders deceased or having otherwise moved on, the Lakeside Laboratory Association, consisting of faculty and supporters, reorganized, amended its Articles of Incorporation, and offered the Station to the State Board of Education (Regents) as a gift (Bovbjerg, Ulmer, and Downey 1974, 9). A legal ruling held that SUI could indeed maintain a field station away from the Iowa City campus without violating the State Constitution (in contrast to what Macbride had been led to believe), and in 1936 the transfer of title occurred. The State of Iowa owned Lakeside Lab in the names of the State University of Iowa and the Iowa State Conservation Commission (later the Iowa Department of Natural Resources).

> The property was to be held in trust for the accommodation, promotion, support and maintenance of scientific studies and research in the field of the biological sciences in connection with the duties and purposes of the Iowa State Conservation Commission and the departments of Zoology, Geology, and Botany of the State University of Iowa. Failure to keep the trust returns the property to its original owners, the Iowa Lakeside Laboratory Association. (Bovbjerg, Ulmer, and Downey 1974, 9)

The Lab was put under the control of five managers, one each appointed by SUI President Eugene A. Gilmore, the State Board of Education (Regents), the Iowa Lakeside Laboratory Association, and the Iowa State Conservation Commission. The fifth manager was to be chosen from the United States Biological Survey by the four other managers. SUI retained control of the Lab, although responsibility was transferred from the Graduate College to the University's Summer School. SUI's Graduate College continued to offer scholarships designed to cover tuition costs. Joseph H. Bodine, head of SUI's Department of Zoology, was appointed director, a position he held in absentia until his death in 1954. Bodine appointed associate directors to represent him at the Lab: L. O. Nolf served from 1934 to 1941, R. L. King from 1942 to 1954.

Lakeside's new status as a State of Iowa institution meant that it was now eligible for federal funding, including FDR's New Deal Programs designed to put people to work to prop up the nation's infrastructure. At that time, Iowa was fortunate in having Henry A. Wallace serving as Secretary of Agriculture (1933–1940) in FDR's cabinet, and Ding Darling serving on the President's Committee for Wild Life Restoration (along with Aldo Leopold and Thomas Beck). As validation for his work on the committee, in 1935 Darling was offered the job as head of the Biological Survey, and he agreed to accept it on a temporary basis (indeed his tenure as director was only eighteen months, when he was replaced by the legendary Ira Gabrielson, a Lakeside alum). After Darling returned to Iowa, he used his influence to reopen the Civilian Conservation Corps (CCC) camp at Milford for the benefit of Lakeside Lab. SUI President Gilmore requested Darling's assistance in getting Lakeside's rating moved up on the U.S. Department of Agriculture's priority list, and Darling in turn appealed to Henry Wallace to reopen the camp. Bovbjerg writes that both Bodine and Nolf helped to persuade Darling to lobby Wallace (Bovbjerg, Ulmer, and Downey 1974, 10).

Approval for the Milford CCC camp reopening came in 1936, and by 1938 Lakeside had four new stone laboratories (Macbride, Calvin, Pammel, and Bodine) and a library and lecture hall (Shimek). These buildings were made with massive, glacially deposited granite boulder walls and topped with cedar-shingled roofs (fig. 14). They were arranged in an arc around the highest hill of the old Floete acreage with the open end facing the lake (fig. 15). Cedars were planted beside each doorway. In addition to these buildings, a stone pump house was built along the lakefront (fig. 16), and four stone cabins and a shower house, all with cedar shingles, were built. An entrance portal to the Station (fig. 17) and stairs to the Pump House were also constructed. The old Floete barn was moved toward the lake, placed on a newly constructed foundation, and converted to the Mess Hall (fig. 18). Below the Mess Hall, toward the lake, CCC workers installed a sanitary system with a large septic tank and extensive tile lines. Bovbjerg writes that these improvements were "tremendous," although the completed project was less than called for in the original plans (Bovbjerg, Ulmer, and Downey 1974, 10). The old laboratory building, with its leaky roof, peeling paint, and rotted sills, was

14. Shimek Laboratory just completed in 1936. The panes of glass still have tape stuck to their lower right corners. This building was the Station's library and office in the late 1930s and through the 1940s and 1950s. When the number of classes started to increase, it became a teaching laboratory. Courtesy of University Archives, Department of Special Collections, University of Iowa Libraries.

15. The Lakeside campus as it appeared in the late 1930s, looking north-northeast from what is now the Presbyterian Camp. This photograph could not be taken today because too many trees have grown in and up. Courtesy of University Archives, Department of Special Collections, University of Iowa Libraries.

16. The shoreline Pump House and, to the right, the stairs, both built by the Civilian Conservation Corps out of glacially deposited boulders. Main Cottage, the original building on the site, sits on the hill above. In the 1960s the Limnology Lab would be cleverly built over the Pump House. Courtesy of University Archives, Department of Special Collections, University of Iowa Libraries.

17. Postcard of Civilian Conservation Corps–built Macbride and Shimek labs, and the massive front gate, likely taken in the 1940s or early 1950s. Today all three structures are on the National Register of Historic Places. This particular postcard was sent from J. R. Murray at Lakeside to Dr. Martin Grant, plant taxonomist and member of the Lakeside faculty in the 1950s and 1960s. Courtesy of University Archives, Department of Special Collections, University of Iowa Libraries.

razed. With new buildings came new responsibilities, and a caretaker, A. C. McKinstrey, was hired. Macbride ensured McKinstrey's first three years' salary was covered, until the Iowa State Conservation Commission could assume this financial responsibility.

In the 1930s Lakeside featured a talented assemblage of faculty, among the best field biologists in the state. Henry S. Conard from Grinnell was the nation's authority on mosses and ran his Moss Clinic out of Lakeside. Iowa Wesleyan Professor H. E. Jacques was compiling his impressive works on insects. SUI Professor Theodore L. Jahn investigated protozoans. In addition to his duties as associate director, Nolf's research in parasitology demonstrated the richness of these pesky animals (nematodes, trematodes, and cestodes) in the Okoboji region. Associate director R. L. King worked out the social structure of ant populations. A major research focus at Lakeside during the 1930s was water quality, especially the "nuisance algae problem" associated with shallow East Lake Okoboji (Bovbjerg, Ulmer, and Downey 1974, 11).

The curriculum underwent minor changes. In 1937 field botany and field zoology were combined into field biology, and protozoology was offered for the first time. Enrollment peaked in 1941, immediately prior

18. The old Floete barn was moved by the Civilian Conservation Corps to a spot overlooking Little Miller's Bay and converted to a mess hall. It is still called the Mess Hall. Courtesy of University Archives, Department of Special Collections, University of Iowa Libraries.

to the Second World War. In 1942 aquatic ecology replaced field biology. Following that summer, Lakeside suspended its summer programs until 1946, although Professor King and others returned annually to continue their research. The postwar course offerings were the same as the prewar offerings: field biology and protozoology.

Other research during this period included: further distributional and life history studies; new species accounts and taxonomic arrangements; descriptions of natural areas including bogs, fens, and pothole wetlands; physical and chemical studies of the lakes; as well as vertebrate anatomical and behavioral studies. New areas of research included nutrient cycling in lakes, prairie and forest restoration, and descriptions of turtle chromosomes. In addition, tests of the piscicide (fish-killing chemical) rotenone were conducted at the Lab. The word "ecology" appears in the titles of several papers (Zieglowsky-Baker 1990, 190–99).

classical state universities
versus land-grant institutions

* *

AS THE CURRICULA of modern universities blend to produce a more homogeneous experience for all, it is easy to forget that there was once a deep division at the collegiate level between the teaching of basic knowledge and instruction in technical knowhow. A hundred years ago in Iowa, students wishing to receive a classic program of study attended the State University of Iowa; if they wished practical training in agriculture, applied science, engineering, or home economics, they attended the land-grant institution Iowa State Agricultural College. Land-grant colleges (later universities) were funded as technical institutions by the federal government, as designated by the Morrill Acts of 1862 and 1890. Iowa State was the first school to receive this federal status, on September 11, 1862. The Hatch Act of 1887 expanded the mission of land-grant universities to provide federal funding for Agricultural Experiment Stations. Forty-five years later the Fish and Wildlife Cooperative Units established by Ding Darling were also housed at land-grant universities.

The names of universities largely give clues to their origins. In many states, land-grant universities have the name State after the state name. As pointed out above, in Iowa the University of Iowa is the classics school, Iowa State the technical school. The same nomenclature occurs in Michigan, with the University of Michigan and Michigan State; in Kansas with the University of Kansas and Kansas State; in Pennsylvania with the University of Pennsylvania and Penn State; in Montana with the University of Montana and Montana State, and so on. Of course, this is not always true. In New Jersey the land-grant school is Rutgers, and in Indiana it is Purdue. In Wisconsin and Ohio, one state university serves both purposes. The same occurs in Minnesota but on two campuses—the Minneapolis campus is classical, the St. Paul campus technical. There are other differences. Classical universities usually host the medical and law schools, land-grant universities the veterinary school. Universities with their origins in the classics tend to be more progressive, while land-grant institutions tend to be more conservative. Such distinctions have diminished today, but origins give insight into approach.

Born from the State University of Iowa, Lakeside's origins are in the classics, in the sciences and humanities. (There was once a summer theater on the Lab grounds, the stage was located where the library is today, and the stands were carved into the hillside rising south to the Macbride Lab. This stage also served as an altar for Sunday morning services.) Early on, enrollments at the Lab reflected enrollments at the university—in 1909 nearly half of Lakeside's students were women. Courses focused on recognizing the diversity of species, learning names, and understanding ecological relationships. Game and nongame species were emphasized. Students were often teachers or on their way to becoming researchers. Small, seemingly inconsequential taxonomic groups received as much attention as species deemed more immediately important to humanity.

Contrast this with the fish and wildlife approach taken by the land-grant institutions. The first fisheries and wildlife biologists focused on commercially important species: muskies rather than minnows, pheasants rather than hummingbirds. Included in the fish and game philosophy were stocking programs designed to artificially inflate wildlife numbers beyond what ecosystems could naturally hold. It was a field dominated by men. The first woman in wildlife biology, Frances Hamerstrom, did not arrive in Leopold's lab until 1940 (and Leopold was progressive). Exceptionally driven and iconoclastic, Hamerstrom had no problem holding her own.

As with the trend toward an amalgamation of university missions, there has been a more recent blending of the basic science and wildlife management philosophies in biology. The best wildlife management practices now incorporate ecosystem management, which includes all the little plants and animals that compose the ecosystems that support game—the organisms that have always been the bread and butter of courses taught at Lakeside. And basic scientists will look beyond game's purely utilitarian functions and use these species to address life's more fundamental questions when they can.

a regents institution

AFTER WORLD WAR II two events changed the course of Lakeside, giving it both breadth and power. The first was a reorganization of the administrative structure. In 1947 director Joseph Bodine wrote a letter to SUI's president Virgil Hancher pointing out the shortcomings of an administrative system where the five managers had no budget to provide for maintenance or operation; instead, each year the director was required to apply to the SUI Summer Session to cover salaries. Bodine proposed that the State Board of Education (today the State Board of Regents) make the Iowa Lakeside Laboratory a Board Institution in the service of the three state universities (UI, ISU, and UNI in current terminology). The Board agreed and acted almost immediately to dissolve Lakeside's Board of Managers and assume provisional control of Lab operations.

In 1948 Bodine laid out his plans for the administration of the Lab, including specific funding earmarked for general overhead, equipment, instruction and research, and caretaker's salary. He proposed a program of quality, not quantity, applied to both teaching and research—he wanted the highest quality undergraduate students, graduate students, and faculty (Bovbjerg, Ulmer, and Downey 1974, 13). The State Board of Education (Regents) accepted these recommendations and later in the year assumed responsibility for the Station. At the University of Iowa the control of the Lab passed from the Summer School to its Extension Division. The Lakeside Laboratory Association was dissolved and its total assets ($4,742.80) were turned over to the State Board, which SUI used through its Graduate School to establish its program of Macbride scholarships. These scholarships provided tuition waivers for qualified students taking courses at Lakeside.

The second event that changed the Lab was slower to develop and likely resulted from Bodine's reorganization—the curriculum began to expand (appendix 1). In 1946 returning veterans and students too young to have served could choose from among field biology, taught by R. L. King, and protozoology, taught by Theodore Jahn, the same two courses offered between 1937 and 1941. In 1948 biology of the mosses was added when Professor Conard returned. This curriculum held through 1951. In 1952 algology and plant taxonomy were added, increasing the offerings to five courses. Algology was taught by John Dodd from Iowa State. Dodd taught algology for an extraordinary thirty-two years (until 1983) (fig. 19). It is easy to see why students loved Dodd—no one had a drier sense of humor. When sampling near wetlands Dodd would advise his students, "Leave no tern unstoned" (MJL, personal observation). Plant taxonomy was covered until 1963 by Robert Thorne and the free-spirited, naturist-naturalist Martin Grant. In 1953 limnology was added to the curriculum; parasitology (later helminthology) began in 1954. The instructor for parasitology, Martin Ulmer from Iowa State (fig. 20), began a twenty-

19. Professor John Dodd (with hat) and students examining plants on what looks to be Cayler Prairie in the late 1950s or early 1960s. Courtesy of University Archives, Department of Special Collections, University of Iowa Libraries.

20. Professor Martin Ulmer examining parasites prepared on microscope slides in the late 1950s or early 1960s. Courtesy of University Archives, Department of Special Collections, University of Iowa Libraries.

three-year run that ended in 1976 when he became the associate dean of the Graduate School at Iowa State. One of Ulmer's favorite things was to comb the labs late at night gathering students. This group would hike south across the Presby beach and up the hill into Wahpeton to Miller's Bay Store for pizza and beer. Ulmer ate more and slept less than most, and could easily handle this excess. For the students, however, a few nights of such overindulgence strung together took a deep toll. Today instructors tell their students: give me the week and I'll give you the weekend (MJL, personal observation).

By 1954 Lakeside offerings consisted of seven courses. Three—field biology, plant taxonomy, and limnology—could be said to be staples of any inland field station curriculum. The other four—protozoology, biology of the mosses, algology, and parasitology—represented a combination of faculty interests and the opportunities for collection and observation that Lakeside offered. Viewed another way, field biology and protozoology reflected past successful course offerings, while biology of the mosses, limnology, algology, plant taxonomy, and parasitology represented trial offerings—new courses that may or may not have been successful. Looking back at this period, biology of the mosses, algology, and parasitology were successful in large part because of the personal and professional appeal of their faculty. Plant taxonomy has always drawn students regardless of the instructor.

In 1955 the curriculum again expanded to include plant ecology and the biology of lower plants. A year later, three new courses were added, including field mycology (fungi), biology of the bryophytes (nonvascular mosses, liverworts, and hornworts), and aquatic ecology, which broadened and replaced the old limnology course. This was the first time mycology had been offered since Macbride's tenure; it was taught during alternate, even-numbered years from 1956 through 2002. The instructor for all this time, Lois Tiffany from Iowa State, was not only iconic—the only woman among Lakeside's current list of distinguished faculty—but beloved.

Richard Bovbjerg was brought in to teach the aquatic ecology course (fig. 21). Bovbjerg was an intellectual of the first class, a former Navy minesweeper skipper who received his Ph.D. after studying with W. C. Allee at the University of Chicago. He taught aquatic ecology at Lakeside for thirty-five years until his retirement in 1989. But more importantly, in 1964 he became director of Lakeside and for the next twenty-six years, much as with his minesweeper, the Station bore the mark of his leadership, which it still does.

From the late 1950s to the mid 1970s the names Bovbjerg, Ulmer, and Dodd reverberated through the laboratories of Lakeside just as Macbride, Shimek, and Calvin had two generations before. King, Conard, Tiffany, Grant, and Thorne were also legendary. As had become the custom, the curriculum consisted of older successful courses and new courses offered based on perceived need or faculty interest; a pattern that has continued to the present.

From 1957 to 1966 courses in ichthyology, plant reproduction, field entomology, diatoms, and Pleistocene landforms were added to the curriculum. The deeply respected John Downey from UNI taught field entomology. The diatoms course (diatoms are a specialized form of algae

21. Professor and former director Richard Bovbjerg taking his aquatic ecology class out to sample West Lake Okoboji in the late 1950s or early 1960s. Courtesy of University Archives, Department of Special Collections, University of Iowa Libraries.

useful to humans in many ways, for example as water-quality indicators and toothpaste additives—diatoms make toothpaste gritty) was started in 1964 by Gene Stoermer, who would take a faculty position at the University of Michigan; two years later Charlie Reimer, of the Academy of Natural Sciences in Philadelphia, took over. Reimer had a global network of colleagues and internationalized the course. After he retired in 1991 Stoermer returned to continue the course, one of the most successful in Lakeside's history. Both Reimer and Stoermer became Lakeside legends—Reimer because of his ability to relate to students, Stoermer for his intellectual presence. Stoermer is the scientist who coined the term "Anthropocene" to describe the current mass extinction of Earth's biota driven almost entirely by human environmental impacts.

At Lakeside, courses quickly develop a routine based on a tentative daily or weekly rhythm. Some courses begin the day inside with some general principle being explained, then go out in the field to observe or demonstrate the phenomenon. Others begin the day with fieldwork, often making collections of plants and/or animals, then move indoors the rest of the day working through identifications. Some courses are in the field several days of the week, then spend other days indoors for lectures and lab work. Most courses offer combinations of approaches because fieldwork can only be done in good weather (no instructor wants to be on a prairie half a mile away from the van when a thunderstorm hits). Because of inclement weather, course syllabuses based on daily routines can rarely be followed throughout an entire session. Goals based on weekly routines, however, can usually be followed and after four weeks, especially with seasoned faculty, all course goals are usually met. Evenings are devoted to studying and activities to unwind; this work-hard, play-hard attitude has always characterized Lakeside. In fact, we on the faculty have found it difficult to sustain the work-hard in our students without the play-hard, although both approaches have their limits.

By the mid 1960s Lakeside's curriculum had settled into a core of nine remarkable courses: field biology, protozoology, aquatic ecology, helminthology (parasitology), algae, plant taxonomy, diatoms, mycology, and entomology (appendix 2). This was a diverse offering backed by a faculty packing plenty of intellectual muscle. Additional horsepower came from the graduate students. Between 1959 and 1974 sixty-eight advanced degrees (twenty-six master of science degrees; forty-two doctor of philosophy degrees) were granted from work done at the Station. Of this total, thirty-three degrees came out of Ulmer's lab, thirteen from Dodd's lab, and ten from Bovbjerg's lab (Bovbjerg 1988, a-7). Throughout the 1960s and 1970s there was continuity at Lakeside from undergraduate students through graduate students to the faculty; intellectual stratification based on academic rank or accomplishment was minimalized, and these easy interactions enriched the whole educational enterprise; a phenomenon commonly observed at field stations but not on university campuses (Janovy and Major 2009, 220–22).

During this period, research at Lakeside included continued studies of species descriptions and taxonomy, life histories and natural histories of plants and animals, species distributions, animal behavior, ecological relationships, parasitology, physical and chemical characteristics of lakes and rivers, invasive plant control, and prairie reconstruction. New research emphases included agricultural runoff, the taxonomy and ecology of diatoms, plant succession, and human impacts on the environment. A prescient 1952 project studied the effects of the herbicide 2, 4-D on mosses.

In the 1970s the combination of limited federal funding opportunities and an increased interest in molecular biology saw graduate participation in Lakeside's programs, indeed field stations in general, wane. This trend was exacerbated when Ulmer was promoted to an associate dean and Dodd retired. While courses in parasitology and algology continued, without Ulmer and Dodd these offerings did not attract students in the same numbers as the originals. Bovbjerg recognized the deep connections between many instructors and their courses. In every sense parasitology and algology were Ulmer and Dodd, and absent their personalities these courses lost their luster.

New faculty included the broad-thinking Robert Cruden and the highly focused Bill Platt from the University of Iowa, who first taught field biology together then split to teach concurrent and successful field botany and prairie ecology courses. Former engineer Larry Eilers from UNI took over the popular plant taxonomy course. Three gifted teachers, Paul Christiansen from Cornell College, Neil Bernstein from Mt. Mercy, and Rick Lampe from Buena Vista, covered field biology under the title field natural history. These courses, too, flourished. Commenting about this period, Bovbjerg wrote (1988, 8):

> Courses which have been consistent and filled over the entire period are aquatic ecology, ecology and systematics of diatoms, plant taxonomy, and field biology (more recently its successor—field natural history). Newer and successful courses include field botany, prairie ecology, field invertebrate and vertebrate zoology, field ornithology and fish ecology.
>
> Some long-lived courses such as field mycology and bryology have persisted with dwindling student numbers. Algology, parasitology, and aquatic plants had a distinguished past but are presently defunct due largely to the retirement of distinguished faculty. Several courses met but once and successfully; they were instances of one instructor with us for one year. Some met once and failed.

New offerings throughout the 1980s and early 1990s included specialty courses such as natural history of the Iowa Great Lakes, developmental biology of the invertebrates (George Brown), neurobiology (Charlie Drewes), and archeobotany. General interest courses included Quaternary studies (Richard Baker), field entomology (Barbara Abraham), field parasitology, and field archeology (John Doershuk) (appendix 3).

Research during this time continued to reflect Lakeside's traditional natural history and life history emphases, but it also incorporated modern ecological thinking in areas such as evolutionary and behavioral ecology. There was an increased emphasis on prairie, lake, and wetland ecosystem studies and the organisms that occupied them, especially vascular plants and their pollination, diatoms, fishes, and amphibians. Parasitology continued to be a research strength; archaeological investigations intensified (Zieglowsky-Baker, 1990, 190–99).

When Iowa State's Arnold van der Valk assumed the directorship in 1994, traditional courses were retained while new course offerings became broader in scope (for example, ecology, evolution, and geology) or more applied (for example, restoration ecology, landscape and environmental planning, watershed processes, and landscape modeling) (appendix 4).

Over the past two decades aquatic ecology, plant taxonomy, diatoms, ecology, plant ecology, prairie ecology, ornithology, and conservation biology have reliably filled. When Bovbjerg retired, the aquatic ecology course was covered by his former student and another Navy veteran, the talented and thoughtful Ken Lang from Humboldt State (fig. 22). When Eilers retired, plant taxonomy was covered by the playfully intellectual Dennis Anderson, also from Humboldt State. Anderson received his plant taxonomy training from Professors Grant and Thorne at Lakeside in the late 1950s. After Anderson retired, personable and hardworking Bill Norris from Western New Mexico State took over. When Reimer retired, Stoermer returned to cover the diatoms course, and now that he has retired, alums of the course—Mark Edlund of the St. Croix Watershed Research Station from the Science Museum of Minnesota, Marina Potapova at the Academy of Natural Sciences of Philadelphia, and Sarah Spalding of the United States Geological Survey in Boulder, Colorado—make up the faculty. The longtime Lakeside veteran Neil Bernstein from Mt. Mercy University now covers ornithology. Plant ecology is offered by the modern-day mountain man Tom Rosburg from Drake. Both Bernstein and Rosburg teach the ecology course. The perceptive and energetic Lee Burras from Iowa State covers both the soils and hydrology courses. When Bill Platt left the University of Iowa, Teddy Roosevelt look-alike Daryl Smith, director of the Tallgrass Prairie Research Center at UNI, took over the prairie ecology course. Until 2002 Lois Tiffany continued to offer field mycology; she was on the Lakeside faculty for forty-six years.

Most observers feel that this continuity—one instructor teaching for decades then passing the torch to their most capable former student or colleague—has formed the backbone of the acclaimed teaching program at the Iowa Lakeside Lab. In the early 1990s former students from courses offered in the 1950s, 1960s, and 1970s were on the faculty. Of course, this tradition gets broken for many reasons, and of course the flipside is also true: faculty with no Lakeside pedigree come onboard who get it right, right away and start a new legacy. One disturbing trend is the dwindling

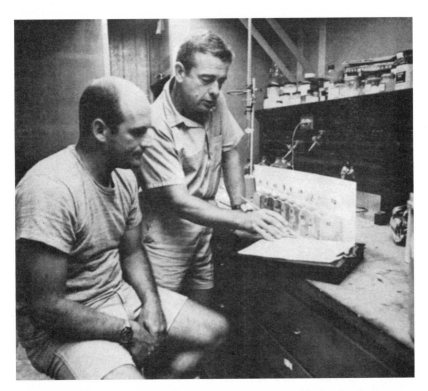

22. Director Bovbjerg and then graduate student Ken Lang considering dissolved oxygen data from West Lake Okoboji in the Limnology Lab in the 1960s. In 1990 after Bovbjerg retired, Lang took over Bovbjerg's aquatic ecology course and continues the tradition to this day. Courtesy of University Archives, Department of Special Collections, University of Iowa Libraries.

number of faculty who are capable of teaching at a field station; the supply of replacements is drying up (Janovy and Major 2009, 221). Back in 1949 Dick Bovbjerg's mentor, W. C. Allee, famously described what has come to be called the Allee effect, where growth rates decline with declining population size; an Allee effect also seems to be occurring within the population of field station faculty.

By the mid 1960s Lakeside's teaching philosophy had emerged, built on Macbride's original ideas, reinforced by Bodine, and formalized by Bovbjerg. This philosophy included (Bovbjerg, Ulmer, and Downey 1974, 17–18):

1   A student body that is small, selected for quality rather than quantity. Students are graduate or advanced undergraduates.

2   Field-oriented teaching and research, with teaching driven by research interests. The courses are field or research extensions of the curricula of the three state universities and do not duplicate campus offerings.

3   A faculty active in research and encouraging project work by students.

4   Courses incorporating complete immersion. Students take one course per term that meets all day, every weekday. [As Bovbjerg often quipped: "Classes and coffee pot start at 8:00 AM and go until drained."]

5   A program consisting of a true collaboration among the three state universities, with each institution providing faculty and students, and the curriculum determined by an inter-institutional advisory board.

Similar to the philosophy at elite universities such as Bovbjerg's alma mater, the University of Chicago, the high faculty-student ratio produced by small class sizes has been a major factor in the success of the instruction at Lakeside. Another factor has been the field nature of every course, with classes outdoors investigating ecosystems for at least a part of every day. The most successful courses have included those taught by faculty immersed in their own research, and the clout of each course has come from the enthusiasm and expertise of its faculty. Because of this approach, the majority of the courses use investigative methods, and discussions often occur through meals and into the evening. Sometimes days are planned, as described previously. Sometimes a class will come across something so profound or unusual that this becomes the course focus for hours or days (fig. 23). This open approach to education mimics the

23. The 2011 conservation biology class learning to field-identify fish at the inlet to Christopherson Slough in northern Dickinson County. Photograph by Susan J. Lannoo.

best of professional life and probably life itself. There are reasons those stone laboratory lights burn bright into the night (Bovbjerg, Ulmer, and Downey 1974, 19).

In aggregate, this approach—dynamic faculty who really know their stuff, small class sizes, emphasis on fieldwork—produces the "lightning in a bottle feeling" described earlier. It is intense, focused, hands-on instruction, and because of the one-course, all-day nature of the curriculum, it is complete immersion. It is a form of education that cannot be duplicated on a university campus (Janovy and Major 2009, 217). The students know this and respond. The loyalty for their parent campus with which the students arrive is complemented by a new loyalty to the Station. This attitude has probably always characterized Lakeside; it certainly persists today (MJL, personal observation).

After Bodine died in 1954, associate director R. L. King took over. Ten years later King stepped down and the University of Iowa aquatic ecologist Richard Bovbjerg assumed the directorship. When Bovbjerg retired in 1989, he had held the position longer than any of his predecessors. Beginning in 1990 the plant pollination biologist and taxonomist Robert Cruden, also from the University of Iowa, assumed the position as interim director and served as a bridge. In 1994 the wetland ecologist Arnold van der Valk became director. Van der Valk was the first Iowa State professor to hold the directorship at Lakeside, and with his tenure the responsibility for the administration of the Laboratory was transferred to Iowa State University. After van der Valk stepped down, Iowa State retained control of the Lab, and Bonnie Bowen took over the newly created executive director position with Cory Petersen as on-site director. For the first time a woman managed the Station.

Each director's administration put its stamp on the Lab. During R. L. King's reign, Bruce E. Mahan, dean of the SUI Extension Division, in cooperation with King, undertook an extensive building campaign. Their goals were to build a new caretaker's home, renovate the old two-room cottages, double the number of cottages through new construction, build a new lecture hall, and install a loft in the Mess Hall. These goals were met, with the lecture hall named for the dean. In addition, the shower house was expanded and the interiors of several of the stone laboratories were modified.

In 1978 Bovbjerg arranged through the state the purchase of an additional tract of land, a 37.5-acre plot located to the east and north of the existing Lab property. This parcel expanded Lakeside's total holdings to about 140 acres, the present-day campus. With this acquisition, Lakeside was bordered to the south by the Presbyterian Camp, to the west by State Highway 86, to the north by Dickinson County's 180th Street, and to the east by residential lots behind Manhattan Beach. The Lab now consists of most of the west and all of the north shoreline of Little Miller's Bay.

Bovbjerg also secured National Science Foundation grants of $21,000 and $62,520 to build the Limnology Laboratory, which was constructed above the old CCC-built Pump House, and the R. L. King Lab (fig. 24), respectively. Both buildings had furnaces and were the first laboratories at the Station equipped for year-round use. An old schoolhouse was purchased from Lakeville Township for $1.00, moved onto the site, and converted to a library. Later, an annex to this library was built with funding from the Macbride estate. A shelter, designed to provide for animals used for observation and experimentation, was built. From 1966 to 1968 faculty cabins were constructed near the site of the first laboratory. In

1972 a pontoon boat was purchased for lake work. Water and sewer systems, as well as the driveways, were upgraded. By 1978 after the Botany (King Lab) Annex was built, Lakeside's physical plant included thirty-five buildings.

Following Bovbjerg's retirement, interim director Robert Cruden, being provisional, had no mandate but advanced the Lab in several ways. First, he understood academic talent and assembled a remarkable faculty (fig. 25). Second, he found money to cover room and board costs, as well as to offer a small budget for faculty keen to arrive before or stay after their courses to conduct research (fig. 26). Third, it was during Cruden's tenure (in 1991) that twelve buildings—Main Cottage and eleven of the twelve CCC-built structures—were placed on the National Register of Historic Places (the Limnology Lab had been constructed over the old Pump House, which disqualified the landmark). And finally, Cruden

24. King Lab in the foreground to the right, and King Lab (Botany) Annex set back to the left in the photograph taken in 2010. The Macbride oak, exhibiting a classic prairie oak shape, occupies the right side of this photo and frames the buildings. Courtesy of the author.

25. Lakeside faculty and associates, 1992. Back row: Kenneth Lang, Dennis Anderson, Nancy Anderson, Susan Lannoo, Robert Cruden, Barbara Abraham, Neil Bernstein, and Debby Zieglowsky-Baker. Front row: Michael Lannoo, Richard Baker, Evelyn Gaiser, and Karen Disbrow. Courtesy of the author.

26. Graduate students Jeff Humphries and Erin Johnson (now Hyde) in 1997 being watched by the local fauna while radiotracking Northern Leopard Frogs on private land, immediately west of the Frieda Hafner Kettlehole, southwest of Lakeside Lab. Courtesy of the author.

oversaw the formation of the Friends of Lakeside Lab (in 1993; see the next chapter). This broad-based group, consisting of business leaders, teachers, and other community members, so reminiscent of the old Lakeside Laboratory Association in mission if not constitution, supported and continues to support the Lab in many important ways. Composed of an impressive number of people with influence and passion representing a cross section of the Okoboji community, Friends has given Lakeside an enormous boost, and their support has been critical (see below).

Following Cruden's administrative bridge, in 1994 Arnold van der Valk assumed the directorship. Van der Valk was able to act upon his many ideas for improving Lakeside, and he was deeply effective. He arranged, through funding generated by the Friends of Lakeside Lab, for the beautiful Waitt Lab to be built—the new building that blends so well with the old CCC-built laboratories and now offers the public face of Lakeside (fig. 27). In the southwestern quarter of the Waitt Lab building, van der Valk established the Bovbjerg Water Chemistry Lab.

Under van der Valk's guidance, the Macbride Laboratory and Mahan Hall were completely remodeled, equipped with central heating and cooling systems, and wired for modern internet capability. The old asbestos-sided cabins were razed or remodeled and several multiroom motel units were trucked in, set on new foundations, and modernized. These units marked the first winterized housing available on campus. Three cottages were moved on site; Tamisiea, Rierson, and Cotton cottages—named for their donors—are used year-round by visiting scholars and other guests. When Iowa State assumed control of Lakeside Lab, building maintenance became a priority; laboratory buildings were upgraded, leaky roofs and sills were replaced, and structures were brought up to code. These repairs were crucial.

Continuity has been provided by the caretaker (since called the resident manager, today called the facilities manager) and his family. The long tenure of A. C. McKinstrey (from the 1930s to 1962) was continued for another four years by his wife Bessie and son-in-law Charles Branstetter, the first resident manager. Branstetter stepped down and was replaced by Bob and Tania Benson (Bob was the resident manager, Tanny the business manager). The Bensons remained until 1978 when they stepped down and were replaced by Mark and Judy Wehrspann.

There is no doubt that the dominant personality of Lakeside during the latter period was Dick Bovbjerg. On the Lakeside faculty from the

27. The Waitt Lab, built in 1996, after the Friends of Lakeside Lab began partnering with the Lab administration to further the educational mission of the Lab. Photograph by Peter van der Linden.

mid 1950s to the late 1980s and director for twenty-six years (1964–1989), Bovbjerg shaped Lakeside's direction more than anyone else. Current director Peter van der Linden—the only director in Lakeside's history who was an alumnus—and two current faculty members (Lang and Lannoo) each took Bovbjerg's aquatic ecology course and were deeply affected. This sort of intergenerational influence has been critical in maintaining Lakeside's traditions. At the same time, Mark and Judy Wehrspann provided the stability—they presided over five directorships of one form or another—and a presence that is best described as family.

While Lakeside's students and faculty count themselves among an international community of scientists and scholars, over the years there has been little that the faculty or the administration, with their relatively short annual residence at the Station, could do to influence land use locally in the Okoboji area. And so, the early twentieth-century swamp-busting activities that swept the Midwest and resulted in Iowa losing 99 percent of its wetlands to agriculture also occurred in Okoboji; the three-wetland complex of Pillsbury, Pratt, and Sylvan lakes (actually permanent wetlands) southwest of the Station was drained, as were nearly all of the little potholes depicted on Shimek's map (see fig. 1). Grasslands faced a similar fate. With the exception of Cayler Prairie, the basin of the Kettlehole, Lakeside's North Forty, and scattered little pocket prairies, all of Okoboji's upland grasslands were plowed for agriculture. The faculty at Lakeside must have wondered each year as they packed their equipment and supplies for the long train ride (later car ride) north, which Okoboji habitats would be still intact and could be visited and which were forever gone.

28. A newly constructed (ca. 1991) seasonal wetland located east of Garlock Slough, built through the U.S. Fish and Wildlife Service's Waterfowl Production Area (WPA) program in association with the Iowa Department of Natural Resources. Courtesy of the author.

And then beginning around 1990, this trend toward habitat loss was reversed. The U.S. Fish and Wildlife Service, through its Waterfowl Production Area program, in cooperation with the Iowa Department of Natural Resources and other fish and game–related organizations such as Ducks Unlimited and Pheasants Forever, began buying farmland and converting it back to wetlands and prairie. The goal in the Okoboji region has been to purchase 30,000 acres and convert the land back to grasslands and wetlands. Today, there are major grassland/wetland complexes in the Spring Run, Welch Lake, Garlock Slough, Kettleson Hogsback, and Excelsior Fen regions (fig. 28). There is now more natural (including restored) habitat in the Okoboji region than there has been since the early 1930s. This is a remarkable accomplishment in today's world, and for those concerned about the future of natural ecosystems, it offers hope. There is even a groundswell of interest in restoring Pillsbury, Platt, and Sylvan lakes. In contrast with their predecessors, Lakeside faculty today pack for the Station and wonder what new habitats they will be able to explore.

the friends of lakeside lab

BY JANE SHUTTLEWORTH

. . . .

IN DECEMBER 1991 the three Regents University presidents recommended that the research and education programs at Iowa Lakeside Lab be discontinued. This recommendation was based on funding cuts imposed on the university system by the Iowa legislature and declining enrollments. Several factors were responsible for the drop in student enrollment. Students increasingly began to own cars, hold summer jobs, and have year-round living quarters while attending college. Enrolling in a five-week summer class at Lakeside meant paying room and board in two locations and losing the opportunity to earn summer income. Another contributing factor at the time was the shift in emphasis from field to molecular biology at the University of Iowa Biology Department.

In response to Lakeside's crisis, local citizens began to organize. Mark Wehrspann, Lakeside's resident manager at the time, and other community members printed leaflets and distributed them in coffee shops around town. This gained the attention of the University of Okoboji Foundation, which formed a Lakeside task force. This task force, led by Sue Richter, Tom Bedell, and Karen Goodenow, entered into discussion with the Board of Regents. They initiated a dialogue among the university presidents, the Board of Regents, and the local community on how to sustain the Lab. They held community meetings, and local residents Eric Hoien and Dave Thoreson created a slide show about the Lab to engage support.

In the meantime, the most immediate crisis—the drop in student enrollment—was addressed by community members who raised scholarship funds. The Okoboji Protective Association, a conservation organization with a long history of informal cooperation with the Lab in water quality and other studies, now intensified its support for Lakeside through a scholarship fund.

. . . .

To address the threat of closing the Lab, the University of Okoboji Foundation's Task Force held a meeting in 1992 with a court reporter to gather public input on the Lab's future. As a result of that meeting, it was believed there was support to proceed with developing a plan to save the Lab. Extensive interviews were conducted with private and governmental groups from the Iowa Farm Bureau, Dickinson County Conservation Board, lake organizations, and government agencies as well as Lakeside alumni and professors.

The meetings among community members, university leaders, and Bob Barak from the Board of Regents office resulted in a three-year plan to improve Lab finances, facilities, community relations, and instructional and research programs. It also included a new governance structure, the Lakeside Lab Coordinating Committee (LLCC), created to strengthen interinstitutional support and ownership of Lab operations. The LLCC included provosts from each university, the Lakeside director, an Okoboji community representative, and a representative from the Board of Regents. Iowa State University became the new host institution for Lakeside Lab.

Historically Lakeside had operated more apart than as an integrated component of the local community. It was open only during the summers, its main purpose to function as a teaching and research institution. It was supported by resources largely outside the local community. The Lakeside crisis of the 1990s and the creation of the Friends, however, brought a new dynamic to the function and funding of Lakeside. The Regents Eight-year Plan mandated the lakes community to increase their financial commitment and support for the Lab. In response, the community requested more opportunities for public participation and a say in determining what those activities might entail.

Two venues for developing and strengthening the community/Lakeside relationship quickly became apparent: the need for a water-quality research program to monitor and analyze the condition of the region's lakes, and the need to expand Lakeside's offerings to year-round and K–12 audiences. At the same time, it became apparent that Lakeside lacked appropriate year-round facilities to meet these goals. This led the Friends to embark on their first project: a million-dollar fund-raising campaign to construct Lakeside's first year-round teaching and research facility, the Waitt Water Chemistry Lab and Teaching Classrooms. Completed in 1998, the Waitt facility was built on schedule and under budget. The completion of this facility allowed the Friends to increase their role in Lakeside's educational programming and water-quality research. New programs made possible since completion of the Waitt facility include:

» Development of public programming: the popular Wild Wednesday programs, guided nature tours, Conservation Conversations, faculty lectures—all in the summer;

» Expanded year-round, seasonally appropriate educational programming for K–12 audiences;

» Creation of various internships and joint programming with groups such as the Dickinson County Conservation Board, the Lakes Art Center, YMCA Camp Foster, and local media internships;

» Development of science teacher workshops and science camps;

» Initiation of a water-quality research program to study sources of nutrient pollution into area lakes and evaluate best-management practices to reduce nutrient input;

» Creation of a citizen lake-monitoring program—the Cooperative Lakes Area Monitoring Program (CLAMP). More than one hundred volunteers from eleven communities in Dickinson and Palo Alto counties in Iowa and Jackson County, Minnesota, have been trained to collect water samples. These data are used in other Lakeside research, and the program is recognized by the Iowa Department of Natural Resources (DNR) as the longest running lake-monitoring program in Iowa. CLAMP data are used by the DNR, the U.S. Environmental Protection Agency, and the Minnesota Pollution Control Agency in water-quality reports as required by the Federal Clean Water Act.

These new programs have broadened Lakeside's audience and outreach to include learners of all ages, including both residents of and visitors to the Iowa Great Lakes region. The water-quality research and monitoring programs have contributed to the creation of a better-informed citizenry and a better-implemented water policy.

a regents resource center

. . . .

WHILE MOST of the traditions inherited from the early days or originating in the past half century have carried through to today, several important administrative changes occurred recently to produce the Iowa Lakeside Laboratory that celebrated its centennial in 2009.

The most important change, the one that has driven all the others, was the 2006 decision by the Iowa State Board of Regents to return the administration of Lakeside to the University of Iowa, specifically back to its Extension Division (today the Division of Continuing Education). Associate provost Chet Rzonca became the University of Iowa's administrative liaison to Lakeside. Concurrent with this move, the Regents appointed an on-site director, Peter van der Linden (fig. 29). For the first time in its century-old existence, Lakeside had a full-time director. Peter, who was a student at the Lab in 1974, arrived after holding administrative positions at Fernwood Botanical Garden and Nature Preserve and the Iowa Arboretum. His charge is to administer Iowa Lakeside Laboratory as a Regents Resource Center.

The expanded goal of Iowa Lakeside Laboratory in its new role is to work with the Friends of Lakeside Lab to develop the presence of the three Regents universities in northwest Iowa. As a Regents Resource Center, Lakeside offers programs in lifelong learning for the people of northwest Iowa. Toward this end, Lakeside is expanding its services. In 2006 the annual Okoboji Entrepreneurial Institute was established to bring undergraduates from the three state universities together with faculty and business leaders. Guided by faculty, students interact with experienced entrepreneurs in an atmosphere of total immersion. This idea of immersion has always been Lakeside's trademark, which is borrowed from the success of its natural history instruction. In 2007 a Writers in Residence program was established. The celebrated Jim Heynen, author of *The Boys'*

. . . .

House: New and Selected Stories (2001), *One Hundred over 100* (1990), and *Sioux Songs* (translations) (1977), has masterfully guided it these past few years with the same goal: immersion of students and faculty by working through ideas. Students write during the morning, with writing centered around a theme often inspired by the Lakeside grounds, and discuss their efforts with Professor Heynen in the afternoon.

The natural history curriculum has also been faring well. The student body has continued its high quality and so has the instruction. Evaluations from a recent Lakeside biology course could have been written in 1909 and included the following comments:

» I love the way in which we were encouraged to learn. Nothing was forced, by any means. [The instructor] made us want to learn for ourselves.

» This is the most I've learned in a class. It was a much better way to learn about the subject matter applicable to my major.

» The freedom [the instructor] gave us in finding our own answers— yet the perspective and advice to know what to look for.

Today, as always, scholarships are offered to deserving students, and an internship program has been developed to offer students summer employment.

29. Lakeside's current director Peter van der Linden, in front of Main Cottage in 2010. Photograph by Tom Jorgensen, courtesy of Peter van der Linden.

In addition to the university curriculum, as mentioned above, Lakeside offers a series of programs designed for both adults and children run by Lakeside's vibrant and tireless education coordinator, Jane Shuttleworth (fig. 30). Adult programs include the faculty lecture series, a weekly public presentation by one of Lakeside's faculty covering their research interests. This is a popular program typically presented to a standing-room-only crowd. Conservation Conversations is a morning program designed to discuss local environmental issues. Often there is a presenter, perhaps from the DNR or other groups with environmental interests, and community members attend. The Coffee and Grounds Committee spruces up the Lakeside grounds. Activities include planting prairie species, weeding the prairie gardens, and harvesting acorns for planting elsewhere in the Lakes region. The Cooperative Lakes Area Monitoring Program recruits citizens (and their boats) in a volunteer effort to monitor the water quality of many area lakes. Nature Weekends, highlighting the area prairies, wetlands, and lake habitats, are popular and draw people from communities across the region. Children's programs include Wild Wednesdays, imaginative evening programs geared to teach children about the environment, and the always filled-to-capacity, week-long Nature Camps, designed around specific themes such as frog camp or eagle camp. During the school year, education programs such as winter botany and life under the ice are geared to K–12 students. Professors from other universities also utilize the Lab, especially during the off-season; 2010 marked the thirtieth year that John Schalles from Creighton University has brought students to the Station to gain field experience in an area with vast ecosystems.

Teaching at Lakeside has not been the only activity where faculty have excelled; their research has also earned wide acclaim. In 1990 Debby Zieglowsky-Baker (190–99) tallied more than four hundred scientific publications resulting from work done at Lakeside. Today, this total exceeds five hundred. There were fourteen papers alone published in association with the Bovbjerg Festschrift, describing research conducted by Lakeside faculty published in a special issue of the *Journal of the Iowa Academy of Science*, and many Lakeside faculty from that era and since have enjoyed active research programs. Faculty have published in international journals such as *Science, Ecology, American Naturalist, American Journal of Botany, The Condor, Journal of Parasitology, Physiological Zoology, Wilson Bulletin,* and *Evolution*, as well as more regional or local journals

30. Lakeside's outreach coordinator Jane Shuttleworth, in her outreach role, in 2010. Courtesy of Jane Shuttleworth.

including the *American Midland Naturalist* and the *Proceedings of the Iowa Academy of Science* (Zieglowsky-Baker 1990, 190–99). Current research interests reflect both past emphases and current trends. Strengths continue to be lake studies, diatom taxonomy and ecology, prairie and wetland studies, amphibian studies, and conservation biology. Soils and hydrology have been new emphases.

Under the University of Iowa's guidance, the Bovbjerg Water Chemistry Lab initiated by Arnold van der Valk is now operating in partnership with UI's State Hygienic Laboratory. The Lakeside facility, run by state chemist Dennis Heimdal, has been certified by the state of Iowa and the U.S. Environmental Protection Agency and can perform a variety of analyses on drinking water, waste water, and surface water for public and private clients.

In 2008 Mark Wehrspann handed over his facilities manager position to Matt Fairchild; in 2010 Judy Wehrspann retired as business manager and was replaced by Ann Ditsworth. In 2010 Matt and his wife Patty welcomed a son Noah. From the 1930s through the early 1950s the McKinstrey family grew up at Lakeside; in the 1960s and 1970s the Benson family grew up at Lakeside; in the 1980s and 1990s the Werhspann family grew up at Lakeside; and now the Fairchild family is beginning its run.

Since Macbride's tenure, Lakeside's directors have consistently lamented the lack of support for building maintenance, but there has been a second neglect that until recently has gone unattended—the Lab grounds. The landscape of presettlement Okoboji was driven by fire. Large prairie fires, whether natural or set by Native Americans, roared hot and fast across the Great Plains grasslands. Shimek's map of the area (see fig. 1) and early photographs (see, for example, fig. 11) clearly show a landscape affected by fires. The only "forests" in the area were on the lee side of large lakes, on peninsulas, or on steep, east-facing slopes; fire-resistant bur oaks predominated. Grazing by large ungulates, especially bison, was also an important factor influencing the vegetation of presettlement Okoboji.

With settlement came fire suppression and the loss of bison. Trees—both native and nonnative species once checked by these influences—became established. What was once open prairie and oak gallery forest became thick, mixed-species woodlands, facilitating the establishment of nonnative invasive species such as garlic mustard, burdock, and bush honeysuckle. Periodically, as faculty interests overlapped with management needs, prescribed fires were set as class exercises, and this activity helped certain areas of the grounds resist woody and nonnative herbaceous invasions. Unfortunately, the lake margins were never burned, and today the densely wooded lakeshore of Little Miller's Bay bears little resemblance to the open prairie landscape of Lakeside's early days. Recently, the Station's new facilities manager, Matt Fairchild, has begun an aggressive campaign to restore the lakeshore and adjacent upland sites to their native, presettlement habitats.

In 2009 the Friends of Lakeside Lab reached their goal of creating a $2 million endowment to assist educational programs and offer scholarships at the Station. As Lakeside rolls into its second century, its financial future now seems secure, and the Lab stands ready to face a new century of environmental issues with new, energized friends and partners.

resurrecting

natural history

* *

AS LAKESIDE contemplates its future, it only needs to look for guidance into its past. The spirit of natural history has always been the strength of both the teaching and the research programs at the Station. And a quick look at the history of course offerings (see appendixes 1–4) shows the detail in which natural history has been emphasized at the Station. From the moment Macbride first stepped into his classroom, courses at Lakeside have emphasized knowing nature in nature.

Eric Engles observed that after World War II the profession of ecology drifted toward specialization, abstraction, theoretical modeling, and reductionism (on-campus activities) (in Lannoo 2010, 143); making it a discipline impossible for the lay person to understand (and easy to criticize). As a result, professional ecology has diminished its capacity as an institution able to influence public policy and, therefore, society at large. Steven Herman (2002, 936) has addressed this situation for a subset of ecology, wildlife biology: "I think the thing [Aldo Leopold] would most lament is the decline of the role of natural history in the study and practice of wildlife biology." Herman elaborates (933), "I find considerable evidence that wildlife management has broken partially free of its roots and is showing signs of malnourishment." Among its problems he includes "addiction to technology [and] lust for statistics." He explains, "The wildlife management discipline [and in fact, ecology in general] started as applied natural history, and most of its star practitioners were broad-based naturalists, intimate with the landscapes and organisms in their charge. There are reasons to believe that the wildlife profession would do well to re-graft itself to those natural history roots." Paul Dayton (2008, 10) continued and broadened Herman's line of reasoning: "Natural history is the foundation of ecology and evolution science. There is no ecology, no understanding of the function of ecosystems and communities, no restoration, or in fact, little useful environmental science without an understanding of the basic relationships between species and their environment, which is to be discovered in natural history."

Today, this emphasis on learning nature in nature is becoming lost. While anthropologists will travel to distant lands to record vestiges of ancient, threatened languages and cultures, at home we are losing equally critical information about our native natural history. There should be an amalgamation of biological disciplines known as heirloom biology that devotes itself to the propagation of natural history disciplines that are undervalued in today's society.

Humankind benefits from a multitude of resources and processes that are supplied by natural ecosystems—including maintaining air and water quality, sequestering carbon, and providing pollinators—that come at no cost to society. Collectively, these benefits are known as ecosystem services, and include the production of food and water, the control of climate and disease, nutrient cycles and crop pollination, and spiritual and recreational benefits (Millenium Ecosystem Assessment 2005). The value of ecosystem services has been estimated at $33 trillion (1997 value), more than twice the total GDP of the world at the time of the estimate (Costanza et al. 1997, 353). These ecosystem services are most often the result of the workings of algae (photosynthesizers), soil and aquatic microbes (decomposers, fertilizers, disease fighters), invertebrates (decomposers, pollinators), and nongame vertebrate species (decomposers, predators, prey)—traditional subjects of the courses offered at Lakeside.

Why should a loss of ecosystem services bother us? Imagine running a $33 trillion business where no one in the company knows how it works. Maybe a few people can name a few parts; only a handful understand how some of these parts work and how they work together. Fifty years ago more people knew more of these things and the business was in better shape, but as experts left they were not replaced. Not only are the threads of life being frayed, but the threads of how to understand life are being frayed.

Today vertebrate populations are being devastated by fungi: amphibians are being wasted by an epizoic chytrid, and bat populations are being wiped out by white-nose disease. For a lack of mycologists—those who study and understand fungi—do we lose amphibians and bats?

When in the late 1980s it was first suspected that trematode parasites cause amphibian malformations, it was not until 2001 when Dan Sutherland (who studied with Martin Ulmer at Lakeside in the late 1970s) became interested that a classically trained parasitologist was on the scene. The quality of the parasitology immediately improved. When Dan died suddenly in 2006, our sadness was mixed with the somber realization that no one was available to take his place.

In 2009 while surveying wetlands on reclaimed coal-spoil prairies in southwestern Indiana, my graduate students and I found a species of fairy shrimp. Only one of us could field-ID it as a fairy shrimp despite a combined twenty-nine years of university education in the biological sciences, and it turned out that there are desperately few people who could identify it to species for us. Fairy shrimp are not common animals in midwestern wetlands and not typically associated with wetlands on postindustrial landscapes. No one could answer why this species was there, or how it got there in the first place.

When public officials decide that a road must be built, they hire consulting firms to survey the proposed route for threatened and endangered species. If these companies employ no experts in biological disciplines (and many do not), what confidence can we have in their reports? For lack of expert advice, what might be destroyed?

There is a species of lungwort lichen, *Lobaria oregana*, that lives in the canopy layer of old-growth Douglas fir forests. These lichens fertilize the forest canopies with nitrogen, which *Lobaria* are able to sequester from the air. *Lobaria* first appear in old-growth forests after about two hundred years, and they do not appear in "big, juicy, drippy abundances" (Preston 2007, 186) until the forest canopy is about five hundred years old. If, in the future, there are no bryologists—no scientists who study mosses, liverworts, and hornworts—will there be anyone who can climb a tree, look at nature, and decipher a story like this? Humans will be better off in immeasurable ways for knowing about *Lobaria* and its relatives.

And there are the crayfish, Dick Bovbjerg's specialty. Crayfish are a keystone species in a variety of upland habitats. Many species of threatened amphibians and reptiles, not to mention large numbers of invertebrates, depend on crayfish burrows, which are dug deep into the ground, to the water table. Without crayfish burrows, these high-profile vertebrates do not survive. Where are the crayfish experts? Turns out there is one: Chris Taylor of the Illinois Natural History Survey. We wish Professor Taylor and all such taxonomic specialists good health and long life, because, as was the case with Dan Sutherland, when we can no longer ask them, there is no assurance we will be able to ask anyone else.

Aldo Leopold has famously said (1966, 190), "To keep every cog and wheel is the first precaution of intelligent tinkering." But we are not just losing the cogs and wheels, we are losing the knowledge necessary to identify them and put them back together again. The larger purpose of the biology program at the Lakeside Lab has always been to know and understand nature's cogs and wheels. Several years ago the Ecological Society of America conducted a survey of their most successful ecologists and found that the one definable constant was field station experience, not the size of their computer's hard drive or the speed of its processor.

In the 1930s the best field biologists in Iowa were said to be on the Lakeside faculty (Bovbjerg, Ulmer, and Downey 1974, 14). With the exception of Paul Errington, who was working out of Ames, this was likely true. This may still be said today, but in fact there are so few field biologists remaining in Iowa (or in most other states for that matter), and many of those who remain are so overcommitted, that Lakeside's administration must frequently go out of state to find instructors to teach its courses. Faculty from the three state universities cover the prairie ecology and soil ecology courses. The ornithology and plant ecology courses are covered by Iowa faculty from the private universities of Mt. Mercy and Drake. The diatoms course is offered by faculty from Minnesota, Pennsylvania, and Colorado. Aquatic ecology is covered by a Californian; plant taxonomy by a New Mexican; conservation biology by a Hoosier. While this diversity of faculty enriches the Lakeside experience, it is telling that most of the people who now interpret the natural history of Iowa at the university level come from outside the state.

Suppose at some point in the future we determine that the no-cost ecosystem services that society depends upon are unraveling along with their host ecosystems. And suppose that we as a society determine that to restore these services we once again need to know the nature of nature. If there is anybody still alive who understands natural history, it is likely they will be working at a field station. It is fascinating to think that the future of humanity as we have come to know it may lie in the information contained in the subjects taught in the many courses offered over the past century at places like the Iowa Lakeside Lab.

Besides the teaching of natural history and the study of the ecological relationships that characterize the world around us, Lakeside has had a second function: as an integrated member of the captivating community of business people, people of faith, artists, thespians, wildlife biologists, and scientists called Okoboji. This area has always been home for an eclectic mix of people—there must be something about the presence of big water that creates or attracts human expression (fig. 31). In a sense, Okoboji is a coastal community built on a lakeshore. Okobojians are people who appreciate the fact that life is not just about business success, or artistic ability, or all that science offers to improve our quality of life; instead it's about all of these. They understand that an integrated life is a

31. Image from the People's Art Project, cosponsored by Lakeside Lab and the Lakes Arts Council, where people assemble into images of animals. In 2010 it was a cardinal. Photograph by Judy Hemphill, used with permission of Judy Hemphill and Joan Gronstal.

full life. Okobojians are people who often send their children to Lakeside and then to the far corners of the world to help improve other peoples' lives and the planet they inhabit. These are big-hearted folks who are secure and comfortable in their own skin, who easily laugh, and who deeply care.

Okoboji's relative isolation from larger population centers has fostered a community independence centered on shared goals; issues based on personal interests that divide less cohesive communities gain little traction here. These are people who always have had only themselves and therefore blame no one else for their troubles.

The Lakeside Lab has helped to form, and in turn has been formed by, this community called Okoboji. And wouldn't it be something if, at the same time Thomas Macbride's Lakeside Laboratory was offering the world the knowledge necessary to understand life's vital little pieces, Okoboji was offering the world the knowledge necessary for small, self-sustaining communities to come together in an integrated way, with a focus on shared interests and a common inclusive vision? Imagine that.

And so those earthy smells in Lakeside's old stone labs conjure not only the spirit of natural history but the more general spirit of a foundation of knowledge based in facts, in inductive, independent, bottom-up thinking. These stone lab spirits are therefore also found, by extension, accompanying grassroots movements and citizen-based organizations formed in response to society's needs. They are there in recycling programs, organic farms, local food initiatives, land trusts—efforts that originate within a community for the benefit of all in the community. They form the basis of what I have called the most powerful idea of the twentieth century: the notion that economies and other societal behaviors must be grounded in ecological principles if they are to be sustainable. In this way, the stone lab spirits may hold the key to the future of humanity; they form the ancient smells that society might wisely heed to remember its way back home.

So many people at Lakeside have influenced me that it is impractical to list them here, so instead I offer my grateful thanks (you know who you are). As for this project, Chet Rzonca and Peter van der Linden gave their approval and supported this effort in several ways such as providing housing and laboratory space while I finished this project, and by offering a publishing subvention. Jane Shuttleworth offered the perspective on the Friends of Lakeside Lab and commented on an early draft. Ann Bovbjerg also kindly commented on an early draft. Peter van der Linden, Sue Lannoo, and Ken Lang proofread later drafts and offered valuable comments. I thank Mary Bennett and Charles Scott of the State Historical Society of Iowa for providing photographs and original surveys of Lakeside and the Okoboji region. I also thank David McCartney and his staff from the University Archives, Department of Special Collections, University of Iowa Libraries for providing access and the rights to reproduce the extensive Lakeside Lab material in their charge. I thank Judy Hemphill, photographer, and Joan Gronstal, president of the Friends of Lakeside Lab, for giving me permission to publish the image from the ArtsLIVE People's Art Project. Look at this photo and ask yourself, who wouldn't want to live there?

APPENDIXES

APPENDIX 1. Course offerings at the Iowa Lakeside Lab, 1946–1966. As you can see, the curriculum expanded, at first slowly and then more rapidly, until by 1964 it reached ten courses offered per summer. The curriculum has hovered around this number, which has generally been regarded as capacity, ever since.

Course	1946	1947	1948	1949	1950	1951	1952	1953	1954	1955	1956	1957	1958	1959	1960	1961	1962	1963	1964	1965	1966
Field biology	•	•	•	•	•	•	•	•	•	•	•	•	•	•	•	•	•	•	•	•	•
Protozoology	•	•	•	•	•	•	•	•	•	•	•	•	•	•	•	•	•	•	•	•	•
Biology of mosses		•	•	•	•	•	•	•	•	•	•	•	•								
Algology							•	•	•	•	•	•	•	•	•	•	•	•	•	•	•
Plant taxonomy							•	•	•	•	•	•	•	•	•	•	•	•	•	•	•
Limnology								•	•	•	•	•	•	•	•	•	•	•	•	•	•
Parasitology (helminthology)									•												
Plant ecology																	•	•	•	•	•
Lower plants										•											
Aquatic biology/ecology											•				•	•	•	•	•	•	•
Biology of bryophytes													•		•						
Field mycology											•	•	•	•	•						
Biology of freshwater fishes												•							•		
Plant reproduction														•							
Field entomology																•	•	•	•	•	•
Diatom clinic																	•		•	•	•
Pleistocene landforms																					•
Total number of courses offered	2	3	3	3	3	3	5	6	7	7	8	8	8	7	8	7	9	8	10	9	10

APPENDIX 2. Course offerings at the Iowa Lakeside Lab, 1967–1983. Note the nearly continuous expansion of new course offerings, as traditional courses were either temporarily or permanently taken off the books. Some courses, such as aquatic ecology and diatoms, were constant through this period. Others, such as field biology, were split into field botany and prairie ecology. In any given year, the number of courses offered ranged from eight to eleven.

	1967	1968	1969	1970	1971	1972	1973	1974	1975	1976	1977	1978	1979	1980	1981	1982	1983
Field biology	•	•	•	•	•	•	•	•	•	•	•	•	•				
Protozoology	•	•	•	•	•	•	•	•	•	•	•	•	•	•	•	•	•
Aquatic ecology	•	•	•	•	•	•	•	•	•	•	•	•	•	•	•	•	•
Helminthology	•	•	•	•	•	•	•	•	•	•	•	•	•	•		•	•
Algae	•	•	•	•	•	•	•	•	•	•	•	•	•	•			•
Plant taxonomy	•	•	•	•	•	•	•	•	•	•	•	•	•	•	•	•	•
Diatoms	•	•	•	•	•	•	•	•	•	•	•	•	•	•	•	•	•
Pleistocene landforms	•		•	•	•	•	•	•	•	•							
Field mycology		•			•					•				•			
Plant ecology		•			•		•			•	•			•		•	
Field entomology		•	•	•	•	•	•	•		•	•	•	•	•	•	•	•
Aquatic plants/botany			•									•					
Field biology of angiosperms				•	•		•								•		
Biology of lower green plants		•			•	•			•								
Floristic botany									•								
Field invertebrate zoology											•	•	•			•	•

Field acarology

Biology of mollusks

Bryophytes & pteridophytes

Ornithology

Field parasitology

Field botany

Endangered species

Prairie ecology

Symbiosis biology

Insect ecology & behavior

Fish ecology

Total number of courses
offered

8 10 10 10 11 9 10 10 10 9 10 11

APPENDIX 3. Course offerings at the Iowa Lakeside Lab, 1984–1994. Note the nearly continuous expansion of new offerings as traditional courses were either temporarily or permanently taken off the books. Courses such as aquatic ecology and diatoms were constant through this period. In any given year, the number of courses offered ranged from eight to eleven.

	1984	1985	1986	1987	1988	1989	1990	1991	1992	1993	1994
Aquatic ecology	•	•	•	•	•	•	•	•	•	•	•
Plant taxonomy	•	•	•	•	•	•	•	•	•	•	•
Diatoms	•	•	•	•	•	•	•	•	•	•	•
Field botany	•	•	•	•	•	•	•	•	•	•	
Prairie ecology	•	•	•	•	•			•	•	•	•
Field vertebrate zoology	•		•	•	•	•	•	•	•	•	•
Field mycology	•		•	•	•				•		•
Aquatic plants / botany	•										•
Field invertebrate zoology	•	•	•								
Ornithology	•						•	•	•	•	•
Fish ecology	•	•	•	•							•
Natural history of Iowa Great Lakes		•									
Field entomology		•			•	•			•	•	•
Bryophytes & pteridophytes		•		•							
Field parasitology		•				•			•		
Field natural history			•	•	•	•	•	•	•	•	•
Field archeology				•		•					
Development of invertebrates					•						
Field mammalogy						•					
Neurobiology							•				
Archeobotany							•				
Quaternary studies							•				
Biology teaching workshop										•	
Algae										•	
Total number of courses offered	11	11	10	11	10	10	10	8	11	11	11

APPENDIX 4. Course offerings at the Iowa Lakeside Lab, 1995–2010. Note the pattern of nearly continuous expansion of new offerings as traditional courses were either temporarily or permanently taken off the books. Courses such as aquatic ecology and diatoms were constant through this period. In any given year, the number of courses offered ranged from seven to eleven.

Course	1995	1996	1997	1998	1999	2000	2001	2002	2003	2004	2005	2006	2007	2008	2009	2010
Aquatic ecology	•	•	•	•	•	•	•	•	•	•	•	•	•	•	•	•
Plant taxonomy	•	•	•	•	•	•	•	•	•	•	•	•	•	•	•	•
Diatoms	•	•	•	•	•	•	•	•	•	•	•	•	•	•	•	•
Prairie ecology	•	•	•	•	•	•	•	•	•	•	•	•	•	•	•	•
Ecology	•	•	•	•	•	•	•	•	•	•	•	•	•	•	•	•
Evolution	•	•	•	•	•	•	•	•	•	•						
Geology	•	•	•	•	•	•										
Plant ecology	•	•	•		•	•	•	•	•	•		•		•		•
Restoration ecology	•	•	•		•											
Vertebrate ecology & evolution	•															
Aquatic plants/botany	•						•	•								
Ornithology	•		•	•		•	•	•	•							
Field natural history	•															
Photography		•														
Field vertebrate zoology		•									•		•		•	
Field mycology		•		•				•								

APPENDIX 4. (continued)

	1995	1996	1997	1998	1999	2000	2001	2002	2003	2004	2005	2006	2007	2008	2009	2010
Fish ecology						•	•	•								
Archeology		•	•	•	•	•	•	•	•	•	•	•				
Landscape environmental planning		•		•												
Conservation biology		•	•		•		•		•		•			•	•	
Biology teaching workshop																
Amphibians & reptiles		•				•		•		•						
Field entomology		•	•		•	•	•	•		•						
Freshwater algae		•	•				•	•		•	•	•				
Plant-animal interactions			•	•												
Watershed processes			•	•									•		•	
Wetland ecology				•	•	•	•	•	•	•						
Freshwater invertebrates				•												
Soil genesis		•		•								•				•
GIS landscape modeling					•	•	•	•	•	•						
Nature sketching						•	•	•	•	•	•					
Amphibians & reptiles (short course)								•								

Behavioral ecology

Environmental planning

Ecosystems

Analysis of
environmental data

Prairie restoration

Astronomy

Writing workshop

Animals & their
ecosystems

Entrepreneurial institute

Total number of courses
offered

13 17 17 16 13 19 14 20 15 15 12 12 8 7 9 9 9

13 17 16 13 19 14 20 15 15 12 12 8 7 9 9 9

Bovbjerg, Richard V. (reviewed and amended by John C. Downey, Bruce W. Menzel, and Robert W. Cruden). 1988. "Status of the Iowa Lakeside Laboratory 1988: Recent History and Assessments." Unpublished manuscript.

Bovbjerg, Richard V., Martin J. Ulmer, and John C. Downey. 1974. "The Iowa Lakeside Laboratory: Its Past, Present and Potential for the Future." Unpublished report to the Graduate Deans of the University of Iowa, Iowa State University, and the University of Northern Iowa.

Brown, Maud. 1910. "The Iowa Lakeside Laboratory as a Student Sees It." *Okoboji Protective Society Bulletin* 5:11–13. Reprinted from Lannoo, Michael J. 1996. *Okoboji Wetlands: A Lesson in Natural History.* University of Iowa Press, Iowa City, Iowa.

Costanza, Robert, Ralph d'Arge, Rudolf de Groot, Stephen Farber, Monica Grasso, Bruce Hannon, Karin Limburg, Shahid Naeem, Robert V. O'Neill, Jose Paruelo, Robert G. Raskin, Paul Sutton, and Marjan van den Belt. 1997. "The Value of the World's Ecosystem Services and Natural Capital." *Nature* 387:253–60.

Dayton, Paul K. 2008. "Why Nature at the University of California?" *Natural Reserve System Transect* 26:7–14.

Hawken, Paul. 2007. *Blessed Unrest: How the Largest Social Movement in History is Restoring Grace, Justice, and Beauty to the World.* Penguin Books, New York.

Herman, Stephen G. 2002. "Wildlife Biology and Natural History: Time for a Reunion." *Journal of Wildlife Management* 66:933–46.

Hodder, Janet. 2009. "What Are Undergraduates Doing at Biological Field Stations and Marine Laboratories?" *Bioscience* 59:666–72.

Jack, H. A. 1945. "Biological Field Stations of the World." *Chronica Botanica* 9(1): 1–73.

Janovy Jr., John, and Krista M. Major. 2009. "Why We Have Field Stations: Reflections on the Cultivation of Biologists." *Bioscience* 59:217–22.

Kohler, Robert E. 2006. *All Creatures: Naturalists, Collectors, and Biodiversity*. Princeton University Press, Princeton, New Jersey.

Lannoo, Michael J. 1996. *Okoboji Wetlands: A Lesson in Natural History*. University of Iowa Press, Iowa City, Iowa.

Lannoo, Michael J. 2010. *Leopold's Shack and Ricketts's Lab: The Emergence of Environmentalism*. University of California Press, Berkeley, California.

Leopold, Aldo S. 1936. "Franklin J. W. Schmidt." *Wilson Bulletin* 48:181–86.

Leopold, Aldo S. 1966. *A Sand County Almanac with Essays on Conservation from Round River*. Oxford University Press, Oxford, New York.

Macbride, Thomas H. 1909. "The Okoboji Lakeside Laboratory." Reprinted in 1985 in *Palimpsest* 66:67–68.

Meine, Curt. 1988. *Aldo Leopold: The Man and His Legacy*. University of Wisconsin Press, Madison, Wisconsin.

Millennium Ecosystem Assessment. 2005. *Ecosystems and Human Well-Being: Synthesis*. Island Press, Washington, D.C.

Moore, Janice. 2010. "Field Stations Introduction." In *Topics in Biological Field Stations*, 1–4. American Institute of Biological Sciences, University of California Press, Berkeley, California.

Preston, Robert. 2007. *The Wild Trees: A Story of Passion and Daring*. Random House, New York.

Simon, Paul. 1967. From the song "Mrs. Robinson." Columbia Records, New York.

Steinbeck, John, and Edward F. Ricketts. 1941. *Sea of Cortez: A Leisurely Journal of Travel and Research*. Viking Press, New York.

Whitesell, Stephen, Robert J. Lilieholm, and Terry L. Sharik. 2002. "A Global Survey of Tropical Biological Field Stations." *Bioscience* 52:55–64.

Wyman, Richard L., Eugene Wallensky, and Mark Baine. 2009. "The Activities and Importance of International Field Stations." *Bioscience* 59:584–92.

Zieglowsky, Debby J. 1985. "Thomas Macbride's Dream: Iowa Lakeside Laboratory." *Palimpsest* 66:42–65.

Zieglowsky-Baker, Debby. 1990. "Eighty Years of Research at Iowa Lakeside Laboratory: A Bibliography." *Journal of the Iowa Academy of Science* 97:190–99.

Abraham, Barbara, 56, 62
Academy of Natural Sciences of Phila-
  delphia, 53, 56
Agassiz, Louis, 11, 12
Allee effect, 5, 58
Allee, W. C., 5, 6, 52, 58
American Museum of Natural History,
  4
Anderson, Dennis, 56, 62
Anderson, Nancy, 62
Anderson School of Natural History,
  11, 12
Anthropocene, 53
Arctic National Wildlife Refuge, 6
Ariss, Bruce, 6
Ariss, Jean, 6

Bailey, Bert, 8, 23, 29
Baker, Debby. See Zieglowsky-Baker,
  Debby
Baker, Richard, 56, 62
Barak, Bob, 68
Beck, Thomas, 42
Bedell, Tom, 67
Benson, Bob, 63, 73
Benson, Tania "Tanny," 63, 73
Bernstein, Neil, 55, 56, 62
Biological Station of the United States
  Bureau of Fisheries, 12
Birge, Edward, 35
Blanchard, Frank, 35
Bodine, Joseph, 41, 42, 49, 58, 59
Bovbjerg, Richard, 5, 12, 40, 42, 52–61,

63, 64, 72, 77; Water Chemistry Lab,
  63, 68, 73
Bowen, Bonnie, 60
Bowen Collegiate Institute. See Lenox
  College
Brown, George, 55
Buena Vista College, 23, 55
Burras, Lee, 56

Cage, John, 6
Calvin, Samuel, 4, 8, 14, 20, 23, 25,
  28–30, 42, 52
Campbell, Joseph, 6
Carnegie Institution, 4
Carson, Rachel, 6, 12
Cherrie, George, 4
Christiansen, Paul, 55
Civilian Conservation Corps (CCC),
  42–45, 60, 61, 63
Clements, Frederic, 4, 5
Coe College, 23
Conard, Henry, 35, 45, 50, 52
Cooperative Lakes Area Monitoring
  Program (CLAMP), 69, 72
Cornell College, 23, 55
Cornell University Biological Station, 12
Cotton Cottage, 63
Creighton University, 72
Cruden, Robert, 55, 60–63

Darling, Ding, 7, 42, 47
Dartmouth University, 7
Darwin, Charles, 11

Dayton, Paul, 75, 76
Dickinson County Conservation Board, 68, 69
Ditsworth, Anne, 73
Dodd, John, 50, 52, 54, 55
Doershuk, John, 56
Dohrn, Anton, 11
Douglas Lake Biological Station, 4, 8
Downey, John, 52
Drake University, 23, 56, 78
Drewes, Charlie, 55
Ducks Unlimited, 66
Dune Laboratory, 11

Earlham College, 5
Edlund, Mark, 56
Eilers, Larry, 55, 56
Eisenhower, Dwight, 6
Errington, Paul, 6, 7, 78

Fairchild, Matt, 73, 74
Fairchild, Noah, 73, 74
Fairchild, Patty, 73, 74
Fernwood Botanical Garden and Nature Preserve, 70
Floete property, 37–39, 42, 45
Friends of Lakeside Lab, 63, 64, 68–70, 74

Gabrielson, Ira, 6, 42
Goodenow, Karen, 67
Grant, Martin, 44, 50, 52, 56
Grinnell College, 45

Hammerstrom, Francis, 48
Hatch Act, 47
Heimdal, Dennis, 73
Herman, Steven, 75
Heynen, Jim, 70, 71
Highland Park College, 23
Hoien, Eric, 67
Humboldt State University, 56

Illinois Natural History Survey, 78
Illinois State (Normal) University, 6
International Union for Conservation of Nature and Natural Resources (IUCN), 6
Iowa Academy of Science, 15
Iowa Arboretum, 70
Iowa Department of Natural Resources (formerly, Iowa State Conservation Commission), 41, 45, 66, 69, 72
Iowa Farm Bureau, 68
Iowa Lakeside Laboratory Association, 16, 18, 19, 32, 34, 37, 38, 41, 49, 63
Iowa State College. See Iowa State University
Iowa State Conservation Commission. See Iowa Department of Natural Resources
Iowa State University (formerly Iowa State College), 4, 7, 23, 31, 47, 49–52, 56, 60, 63, 68; Fish and Wildlife Cooperative, 7
Iowa Wesleyan University, 23, 45
Itasca Field Station, 4, 8

Jacques, H. E., 45
Jahn, Theodore, 45, 50
Juday, Chauncy, 35

Kansas State University, 47
Kay, George, 8, 23, 29, 31
Keyes, Charles, 31
King, R. L., 42, 45, 46, 50, 52, 59, 60; Lab, 60, 61

Laboratory of Marine Zoology and Physiology, 11
Laboratory of the Marine Biological Association, 11
Lakes Art Center, 69
Lakes Art Council, 79
Lakeside Lab Coordinating Committee, 68

Lampe, Rick, 55
Lang, Ken, 56, 57, 62, 64
Lenox College, 14, 23
Leopold, Aldo, 4–7, 42, 48, 75, 78
Leopold, Nina, 5

Macbride, Thomas, 4, 8, 9, 14–16, 18–20,
   23, 25, 28, 30–38, 41, 42, 45, 49, 52,
   58, 60, 61, 74, 75, 80; lab, 44, 48, 63;
   scholarships, 49
Maclean, Norman, 7
Mahan, Bruce, 60
Mahan Hall, 63
Marine Biological Laboratory at Woods
   Hole, 11
Martin, George, 33–35, 40
McKinstrey, A. C., 45, 63
Michigan State University, 47
Miller, Henry, 6
Minnesota Pollution Control Agency, 69
Montana State University, 47
Morningside College, 6, 23
Morrill Acts, 47
Moss Clinic, 38
Mountain Laboratory of the University
   of Utah, 12
Mt. Mercy University, 55, 56, 78
Murie, Adolph, 5
Murie, Mardy, 5, 6
Murie, Olaus, 5, 6
Myerly properties, 36–38

National Science Foundation, 60
Nolf, L. O., 42, 45
Norris, Bill, 56
North Dakota State University, 5

Ohio State University, 47
Okoboji Entrepreneurial Institute, 70
Okoboji Protective Association, 67

Pacific University, 5
Pammel, Louis, 31; lab, 42

Parsons College, 23
Penn State University, 47
Peterson, Cory, 60
Pheasants Forever, 66
Platt, Bill, 55, 56
Potapova, Marina, 56
Prairie Coteau, 6
Prescott, G. W., 40
Purdue University, 47

Regents of Iowa State Board of Educa-
   tion, 23, 41, 49, 67, 68, 70
Regents Resource Center, 70
Reimer, Charlie, 53, 56
Richter, Sue, 67
Ricketts, Ed, 5–7, 9
Rierson Cottage, 63
Roosevelt, Franklin Delano (FDR), 42
Roosevelt, Theodore, 4, 8, 15, 56
Rosburg, Tom, 56
Royal Hungarian Marine Biological
   Station, 12
Rutgers University, 47
Rzonca, Chet, 70

Schalles, John, 72
Schmidt, Franklin, 4
Schmidt, Karl, 5
Science Museum of Minnesota, 56
Shimek, Bohumil, 4, 8, 14–16, 23, 28–32,
   35–38, 40, 42, 52, 74; lab, 43, 44
Shuttleworth, Jane, 67–69, 72, 73
Simpson Centenary, 23
Smith, Daryl, 56
Smith, G., 40
Smithsonian Institution, 15
South Dakota University, 6
Spaulding, Sarah, 56
St. Croix Watershed Research Station,
   56
Steinbeck, Carol, 6
Steinbeck, John, 6, 7, 9
Stephens, T. C., 30, 31

Stoermer, Gene, 53, 56
Stromsten, Frank, 32, 33, 38, 40
Sutherland, Dan, 77, 78

Tabor College, 23
Tallgrass Prairie Research Center, 56
Tamisiea Cottage, 63
Taylor, Chris, 78
Thoreson, David, 67
Thorne, Robert, 50, 52, 56
Tiffany, L. H., 40
Tiffany, Lois, 52, 57

Ulmer, Martin, 50–52, 54, 55, 77
University of Chicago, 5–7, 52, 58
University of Iowa, 8, 14, 22, 23, 30,
    32–34, 38, 41, 45, 47–49, 55, 56, 59,
    60, 67, 73; alumni, 8, 9, 16, 18, 19, 22,
    24, 32, 38; Continuing Education,
    70; Extension, 49, 60; State Hygienic
    Laboratory, 73
University of Kansas, 47
University of Michigan, 4, 5, 8, 35, 47, 53
University of Minnesota, 4, 8, 47
University of Montana, 47
University of Nebraska, 4
University of Northern Iowa (UNI), 49,
    52, 55, 56
University of Okoboji Foundation, 67,
    68
University of Pennsylvania, 47
University of Utah, 12
University of Wisconsin, 5, 35, 47

Upper Iowa University, 23
U.S. Biological Survey, 5, 6, 41, 42
U.S. Clean Water Act, 69
U.S. Environmental Protection Agency,
    69, 73
U.S. Fish and Wildlife Service, 6, 65, 66;
    Waterfowl Production Area, 65, 66
U.S. Forest Service, 5
U.S. Geological Survey, 56

van der Linden, Peter, 64, 70, 71
van der Valk, Arnold, 56, 60, 63, 73

Waitt Lab, 63, 64, 68, 69
Wallace, Henry, 42
Wehrspann, Mark, 63, 64, 67, 73, 74;
    Judy, 63, 64, 73, 74
Western New Mexico State University,
    56
Wilderness Society, 6
Wildlife Management Institute, 6
Woods Hole Oceanographic Institute, 12
World Wildlife Fund, 6
Writers in Residence Program, 70
Wylie, Robert, 8, 23, 25, 28, 30, 32–34, 40

YMCA Camp Foster, 69

Zieglowsky, Debby. *See* Debby
    Zieglowsky-Baker
Zieglowsky-Baker, Debby, 14, 34, 62, 72
Zoological Station of Naples, 11

The Biographical Dictionary of Iowa
    Edited by David Hudson, Marvin Bergman, and Loren Horton

The Butterflies of Iowa
    By Dennis W. Schlicht, John C. Downey, and Jeffrey Nekola

A Country So Full of Game: The Story of Wildlife in Iowa
    By James J. Dinsmore

Deep Nature: Photographs from Iowa
    Photographs by Linda Scarth and Robert Scarth, essay by John Pearson

The Elemental Prairie: Sixty Tallgrass Plants
    Paintings by George Olson, essay by John Madson

The Emerald Horizon: The History of Nature in Iowa
    By Cornelia F. Mutel

Enchanted by Prairie
    By Bill Witt and Osha Gray Davidson

Fifty Common Birds of the Upper Midwest
    Watercolors by Dana Gardner, text by Nancy Overcott

Fifty Uncommon Birds of the Upper Midwest
    Watercolors by Dana Gardner, text by Nancy Overcott

Forest and Shade Trees of Iowa: Third Edition
    By Peter van der Linden and Donald Farrar

Fragile Giants: A Natural History of the Loess Hills
    By Cornelia F. Mutel

Frontier Forts of Iowa: Indians, Traders, and Soldiers, 1682–1862
    Edited by William E. Whittaker

An Illustrated Guide to Iowa Prairie Plants
    By Paul Christiansen and Mark Müller

The Indians of Iowa
    By Lance Foster

An Iowa Album: A Photographic History, 1860–1920
    By Mary Bennett

The Iowa Nature Calendar
    By Jean C. Prior and James Sandrock, illustrated by Claudia McGehee

Iowa's Archaeological Past
    By Lynn M. Alex

Iowa's Geological Past: Three Billion Years of Change
    By Wayne I. Anderson

Landforms of Iowa
By Jean C. Prior

Man Killed by Pheasant and Other Kinships
By John T. Price

Okoboji Wetlands: A Lesson in Natural History
By Michael J. Lannoo

Prairie City, Iowa: Three Seasons at Home
By Douglas Bauer

Prairie in Your Pocket: A Guide to Plants of the Tallgrass Prairie
By Mark Müller

Status and Conservation of Midwestern Amphibians
Edited by Michael J. Lannoo

Stories from under the Sky
By John Madson

*Sunday Afternoon on the Porch: Reflections of a Small Town
in Iowa, 1939–1942*
Photographs by Everett W. Kuntz, text by Jim Heynen

A Tallgrass Prairie Alphabet
By Claudia McGehee

Up on the River: People and Wildlife of the Upper Mississippi
By John Madson

Where Do Birds Live?
By Claudia McGehee

Where the Sky Began: Land of the Tallgrass Prairie
By John Madson

Wildflowers of the Tallgrass Prairie: The Upper Midwest
By Sylvan T. Runkel and Dean M. Roosa

A Woodland Counting Book
By Claudia McGehee